DATE DUE

Black Freemasonry
and Middle-Class Realities

University of Missouri Studies LXIX

Black Freemasonry
and Middle-Class Realities

Loretta J. Williams

University of Missouri Press

Columbia & London, 1980

Copyright © 1980 by
The Curators of the University of Missouri
University of Missouri Press, Columbia, Missouri 65211
Library of Congress Catalog Card Number 79– 48029
Printed and bound in the United States of America
All rights reserved

Library of Congress Cataloging in Publication Data
Williams, Loretta J. 1937–
    Black Freemasonry and Middle-Class Realities
    Bibliography: p. 139
    Includes index.
    1. Freemasons, Afro-American—History. I. Title.
HS883.W54   366'.1'0973   79– 48029
ISBN 0– 8262– 0308– 6

Selections from *Slaves Without Masters: The Free
Negro in the Antebellum South, copyright* © 1974
Pantheon Books, Inc. Reprinted by permission.

Acknowledgments

That the subject of Prince Hall Freemasonry should intrigue me over the years is a credit to the existence of a strong and affirmative black community that nurtured my realization of the responsibilities of self and community development. I owe a deep debt to my father, Leon Gerryfield Lomax, who, while not sharing Masonic secrets with a female child, taught me the importance of Masonic commitment to social justice. My mother, Ira Graves Lomax, taught me well to enjoy the joys of a persistently inquring mind. Only in my maturity have I come to realize the truly good fortune I have had in being their daughter.

Theos, Kenelm, and Kyle McKinney, my delightfully strong sons, have provided encouragement in multiple ways and sustained us through all the various stages of my research career. Their patience and caring has been without bounds.

It is with deep appreciation that I acknowledge the funding assistance of Black Analysis, Inc., New York, and the National Fellowships Fund. The opportunity to share in the development of greater understanding of the experiences of and for blacks in America with BAI members and fellows has proved invaluable.

The faith of so many persons—Ernest Rice McKinney, William J. Wilson, Mark van de Vall, George Silcott, Michael Thorn, and others—is gratefully acknowledged.

L. J. W.
February 1980
Columbia, Missouri

Contents

1. Introduction, *1*

2. The Emergence of Prince Hall
   Freemasonry, *10*

3. The Free Black Context, *21*

4. Nineteenth-Century Realities
   for Free Blacks, *28*

5. The Growth of Prince Hall
   Freemasonry, *38*

6. The Masonic Realities, *47*

7. The Discrepancy in Universalism:
   Minorities, *60*

8. Black Association:
   Pragmatic Adaptation?, *78*

9. The Commitment of Black Masons, *89*

10. The Middle-Class Phenomenon, *103*

11. Implications of Pillarization, *128*

Appendix: Methodology, *135*

Bibliography, *139*

Index, *157*

*Black Freemasonry
and Middle-Class Realities*

Chapter 1

Introduction

Throughout American history, from colonial times through later periods, black Americans have reluctantly faced the fact of their exclusion from the mainstream of American life. This experience of reaction and adjustment has been particularly painful for the members of the black middle classes—those who have held fast to the "American dream," believing that the rewards of hard work and struggle would be success in the literal sense of the word. This book documents some of the realities of success as being racially delimited. For more than two hundred years this segment of the black middle class has at the same time dealt with the system of exclusion and yet achieved some of the system's proffered rewards.

It is the story of the Prince Hall Masons, an organization within the black community established over two hundred years ago. By examining this black organization, from the colonial period to the present, one can more fully understand the struggles of the black, middle-class men. Black Freemasonry, as a separate structure, emerged in response to the discriminatory practices and policies of mainstream American Freemasonry, an institution dedicated to the universal brotherhood of mankind.

This analysis also presents a sociohistorical perspective on black communities and matters of racial segregation, one highlighting the reaction of minority achievers to barriers, their reactions to disillusionment, and the perseverance of hope. In the process, a commentary emerges on the general ignorance, academic and public, of the true history of black Americans.

The black experience is part and parcel of American history. The achievements of black Americans under conditions of great inequality represent a classic picture of the potential of, and for, such achievement under adversity. Is it not an American success story that blacks have persevered, advanced, and survived as a corporate body?

The fact that institutions within the black community have

been invisible to many eyes does not negate the facts of history. Sociological analyses of community and institutional contexts of Prince Hall Freemasonry, and other black institutions not here discussed, document the presence and function of black achievers in a paradoxical environment. The longevity of this organization within black communities, the commitment it engenders in its members, and the effectiveness of its operation make Prince Hall Freemasonry a fascinating story.

This book serves also to highlight the extreme diversity within the black community[1] and sharpens a realistic portrayal of the evolving concerns of the black middle class. Library shelves have recently bulged with stories of the heroism of black pioneers: the Sojourner Truths, the Benjamin Bannekers, the Martin Luther Kings. Alongside have come the analyses of conditions and consequences of oppression and the descriptive interpretations of caste and class stratification. While there are a growing number of publications on the so-called black experience, black Freemasonry, despite the considerable impact, durability, and numbers of blacks participating, tends to reserve little attention.

The story of Prince Hall Freemasonry, which draws its membership from the middle strata of a minority community, mirrors the varied experiences of the American black. In developing a perspective on black Freemasonry, and the context from which it emerged and flourished, one gains insight into the free black male experience in colonial America and the new nation, the growth and socioeconomic history of the black middle class, the structuring of the black community in general, and the occupational and educational endeavors of a certain segment of the black population. It is especially important to recognize the opposition to the situation of devalued status in America despite individual and collective achievements.

In addition, the story of Prince Hall Freemasonry raises intriguing questions about the fraternal order of Freemasonry worldwide. This mainstream fraternity of select and selected individuals teaches "monotheism, morality and immortality" by symbolism and encourages faith in the Diety and the power of

---

1. The term *black community* is used here for simplicity. There is, of course, no such thing as the *black community*. There are instead a number of common patterns of interactions and institutions among varied mixture of persons of Afro-American descent in the United States.

committed friendship.[2] While functioning under the seal of secrecy, the members perfect their civic virtues and moral principles, a perennial though prosaic task.[3] No longer the mysterious secret society of yore, Freemasonry is a society with certain secrets.

One secret now becoming more visible is the exclusionary practices, past and present, of mainstream Freemasonry.[4] The history of Freemasonry's relations with minority groups, whether black, Jewish, or Mormon, reflects social patterns of minority group discrimination: "The history of Masonic emancipation is a mirror clearly reflecting the problems inherent in civil emancipation."[5] Examination of black Freemasonry allows one to explore the theoretical implications of this paradoxical phenomenon of racial separatism within an ideological brotherhood based upon the values of equality, fraternity, and humanism. Analyzing the perpetuation of this specific institutional pattern will shed light on the phenomenon of separate, parallel organizational forms deeply rooted within the black community.

Freemasonry is commonly accepted as the most imitated of all fraternal organizations. Its importance stems from the fact that its nature, character, ritual, and function appear to have formed the basis, directly or indirectly, of every secret society and fraternal order since the eighteenth century. Masons, presently constituting a geographically dispersed membership of over six million males throughout the world, pledge themselves to common beliefs and actions. As within every social world, there is a special universe of discourse, a particular manner of categorizing experiences, a unique set of symbols and referents, and a general worldview. Freemasonry is the largest fraternal order in the world.[6]

But does that include black adherents to the Masonic worldview? Central to the question is the existence, and nonrecognition by mainstream Freemasonry, of a category within the brotherhood that appears to be beyond the pale of idealistic brotherhood: black Freemasons. Prince Hall Freemasonry

2. J. M. Roberts, *The Mythology of the Secret Societies*, p. 30.
3. Melvin M. Johnson, *The Beginnings of Freemasonry in America*, p. 23.
4. Alvin J. Schmidt and Nicholas Babchuck, "The Unholy Brotherhood: Discrimination in Fraternal Orders," *Phylon*, p. 275.
5. Jacob Katz, *Jews and Freemasons in Europe 1723–1939*, p. 4.
6. James Dewar, *The Unlocked Secret: Freemasonry Examined*, p. 47.

exactly duplicates in style and form the more visible mainstream American variety of Freemasonry.[7]

How, then, did the founders of this parallel institution come to Freemasonry, and with what expectations? Did not the ideological contradiction inherent in discriminatory treatment within a universal brotherhood become apparent and remain apparent over the decades? How have black Masons resolved this dilemma? Given that Prince Hall Freemasonry was the first black institution organized nationwide and that it remains strong with over a half million black males as members, one must examine the reality and dilemmas of attraction to Freemasonry. The specific attractiveness of the institution for blacks and other minority groups appears to stem from the perceived nature and impeccability of its goals, works, reputation, secrecy, status, and social power.

Some would argue that black Masons have been beset with internal dissensions and that Prince Hall Freemasonry is merely an assimilationist response of bourgeoisie-oriented elites.[8] Existing documentary evidence suggests otherwise, and this aspect, found from time to time in local situations, is no more marked than in other voluntary associations, white or black. It reveals a fascinating history of black middle-class males integrally involved in the affairs of the evolving community and society.

The phenomenon of Prince Hall Freemasonry provides suggestive insight into certain modes of minority adjustment. It appears that while a subordinate group, in this case racial, will attempt to offset negative definitions of itself by accentuating unique cultural and behavioral achievements, the greater the group's dependence upon the superordinate group for survival and success, the more it will pattern itself after the latter in an attempt to gain access to societal rights and privileges. This investigation attempts to explore this general statement.

The basic assumption underlying this study is that members

---

7. The term *mainstream* will be used throughout as synonymous with *white American*. The term encompasses a broader aspect than skin color: the power, prestige, and privilege accorded by virtue of established patterns of interaction.

8. William A. Muraskin, *Middle Class Blacks in a White Society: Prince Hall Freemasonry in America.*

of the black middle class in the United States have been, and are, subject to status incongruity, strains due to discrepancies in status related to their being, simultaneously, achievers occupationally and socioeconomically, and members of a group stigmatized due to racial ascription as being of lower social status.

In general, recent sociological approaches to minority-status incongruity have focused upon the more visible militant responses to the strains inherent in minority status.[9] This mode of resolution, however, is only one of several possible adaptive stances. The earlier literature on black communities placed greater emphasis on another form of adaptation to minority status and its inconsistencies: the impact and satisfaction of the "brotherhood of religion."[10] Each of these modes of adaptation explains certain aspects of the black community, but neither fully addresses the reality of a third pattern of adaptation, one found particularly prevalent within the black middle class.

Membership in fraternal organizations has been of even greater import in the daily lives of blacks than the respected religious institutions. The character and reputation of each organization to which one belongs, and the number of these in many instances, provide a major basis for one's community status and prestige.

The contribution of black Freemasonry to the needs, basic and acquired, of its constituent members is explored in this study; further analysis attempts to examine the contribution of black Freemasonry to the larger social systems within which it is embedded: Freemasonry, American society, the local community, and the black community. What has been the extent of participation of black Masons in efforts for greater civil, economic, and social rights for blacks?

The stability of the biracial social structure of American Freemasonry will be discussed, for the black Masons of today have adapted, in perhaps different ways, to the mainstream

9. James A. Geschwender, in "Status Inconsistency, Social Isolation and Social Unrest," *Social Forces,* argued that such imbalances in status lead to status disequilibrium that may be resolved in revolutionary activity.

10. See, for example, August M. Meier, "Negro Racial Thought in the Age of Booker T. Washington, 1880–1915," Ph.D. diss., Columbia University, 1957; Saunders Redding, *They Came in Chains;* see also *The Journal of Negro History* (1916–), particularly the early years when edited by its founder, Carter G. Woodson.

rejection of the philosophical requirements of Freemasonry. Since 1827, Prince Hall Masons have declared their independence from mainstream Masonry in the United States. The black Masons have rarely, and never in the twentieth century, asked for amalgamation with the white body; in fact, they would reject it. Pride in the historic black institution is repeatedly stressed, as is disdain for the moral lapse and "colorphobia" of white Freemasonry. Black Masons contend that white Masons have obscured the "true and plain" meaning of Masonic brotherhood, injecting "all their prejudices and their 'beautiful abstraction,' by which evasion can be kept up."[11]

In adapting to exclusionary practices by whites, blacks have come to value their own autonomy highly. Masonic recognition, rather than Masonic integration, is necessary, black Masons maintain. Evidence suggests that concerns over breaking the proud tradition of the black organization obviate any desire to become assimilated within the larger body.

Sociological literature is slowly but increasingly reflecting an awareness that, within the context of the social system, ethnicity is a far more complex variable than has been assumed.[12] Instead of the assimilationist model of increased dilution of original cultural practices as American traits and behavior take over, the modern scene is viewed as reflective of a move to expanding particularism. The pluralist model is being increasingly refined to include the structural factors that have maintained ethnic identity. With the aim of further refining the pluralist model, we explore the theoretical implications of this paradoxical phenomenon of racial separatism.

The phenomenon of similarity combined with separateness, as in Freemasonry, is interpreted as an example of the structural principle of pillarization. The concept is borrowed from discussions by Johan Goudsblom on the nature of parallel forms of social groupings and institutions within Dutch society.[13] Analyzing Dutch society over the centuries, Goudsblom highlighted

11. Arthur A. Schomburg, "Freemasonry Versus 'An Inferior Race': Rejoinder Made to Recent Article by One Who Speaks for Negro Masonry," Harry A. Williamson Collection, Schomburg Library, n.d.

12. William L. Yancey, Eugene P. Erickson, Richard N. Julian, "Emergency Ethnicity: A Review and Reformulation," *American Sociological Review*, pp. 391–403; Orlando Patterson, *Ethnic Chauvinism: The Reactionary Impulse*.

13. Johan Goudsblom, *Dutch Society*.

the various *zuilen,*[14] multifunctional social groupings as mechanisms for maintenance of peace and harmonious functioning between religious factions. Dutch society, until recently, had been composed of four basic institutional groupings along religious lines. Each *zuilen* consists of parallel sets of organizations and institutions: education, politics, recreation, trade unions, media channels, and social clubs. According to Goudsblom, the Calvinist, Catholic, Socialist, and Conservative pillars, each rooted in its own social base, formed the foundation of Dutch social structure.

Others have examined the phenomenon of formal organizations among ethnic groups taking the form of one existing in the dominant culture.[15] It is useful to develop the concept of pillarization to interpret the phenomenon of similarities based on functional principles: the efficient attainment of organizational goals combined with separateness based on nonfunctional principles; that is, race and religion. While its major purpose may be to lessen the subordinate group's institutional dependence upon the dominant group, pillarization may become an emancipatory device that leads to greater autonomy for the subordinate group. In the Dutch instance this did occur. Two religious minorities, Orthodox Calvinists and Roman Catholics, united around the issue of a threat to the continuance of religious institutions in the Dutch schools. In the political and economic sectors this led, in major part, to viable political parties and labor unions grounded upon religious affiliation.

14. Pillarization is taken from the Dutch term *Verzuiling,* which literally means social segregation along the principle of institutional columns or pillars. See Loretta J. Williams, "Pillarization as an Analytic Tool in Race Relations," unpublished manuscript. An intellectual debt is owed to postwar Dutch sociology, which initially analyzed the pillarization phenomenon. See Goudsblom, *Dutch Society*; Arend Lijphart, *The Politics of Accommodation: Pluralism and Democracy in the Netherlands.* There is a similarity in concept to Schermerhorn's "institutional pluralism" in R. A. Schermerhorn, *Comparative Ethnic Relations,* and Milton Gordon's "structural pluralism" in *Assimilation in American Life.* However, the term *pillarization* is better suited to capture the power dimension inherent in parallel organization systems.

15. See Raymond J. Breton, "Ethnic Communities and the Personal Relations of Immigrants," Ph.D. diss., The Johns Hopkins University, 1961; Val R. Lorwin, "Segmented Pluralism: Ideological Cleavages and Political Cohesion in the Smaller European Democracies," *Comparative Politics,* pp. 141–75.

The pillarized religious groups worked through their mutual antagonism to segmented integration for equitable input into social decisionmaking. Can partial pillarization be a mechanism for maintaining harmonious and equitable functioning in an increasingly racially polarized society?

The institutional superstructure of the black community documents strong viable organization: black religious bodies, black educational institutions, black newspapers and radio stations, black civic groups, and black voluntary association. In the United States, formal and informal contacts have traditionally been defined by racial ascription, the most salient criterion for social differentiation in our country. In both Dutch and American societies, one dimension of status ranking has had major impact upon the degree and type of social and cultural participation. This is not to say that other factors have not contributed to stratification ranking. However, in both societies one dimension has had the highest institutional impact.

In both social systems, pillarization occurred in response to historical circumstances. In the United States it was the barring of admission of blacks in the existing societal institutions. As a pragmatic response to their subordinate status, blacks, free and slave, established, or had established for them, separate educational, religious, civic, and social institutions that were often parallel in goal and form to those existent in the dominant society. These institutions arose during the late eighteenth and early nineteenth centuries, most notably in response to castelike segregation. They offered a means to cope with the glaring gap between the reality of interpersonal and intergroup behavior in our society and the democratic values upon which the country was founded. With the decline of legalized caste systems, though by no means the consequences of such, and slow movement in the direction of greater equality, one notes the maintenance or continuance in development of such parallel institutions. The questions arise: What are the factors surrounding this phenomenon? Is it caste enclosure as before? Or is it autonomy now rather than in previous times? One finds not only racially segregated neighborhoods but parallel religious and social forms in each of the racially distinct social systems. In other words, American society can be analyzed in terms of a pillarization process along racial lines having major impact upon all social division. Given the continued politicized use of ethnicity, and the increasing collective self-consciousness of blacks in the past two decades, will pillarized institutions come to exercise an increasing impact on the continuous structuring of interaction in our society?

This study of Prince Hall Freemasonry can only begin the search for answers to such questions. It is viewed as a move in the direction of greater understanding of the diversity within the black community, a social history of one long-standing institution within the black community. It is also a sociological analysis of the response patterns of one segment within the American black population, a segment that is impressionistically known to have many layers and strata within its boundaries: the black middle class. Black Freemasonry, middle-class in orientation and membership, emerged as a practical and rational response to the situation of minority devaluation and the particularly conflictful context for minority achievers. It has been an attempt by middle-class black males to present evidence that identification with, and commitment to, societal institutions valued in the larger society existed in the minority community. Further, black Freemasonry has served as an insulator against the stressful aspects of marginality potentially experienced by individuals with status inconsistencies.[16]

16. Status inconsistency occurs when the correlation between one's various rankings of status dimensions is low.

Chapter 2

The Emergence of
Prince Hall Freemasonry

When the English settlers came to the shores of the New World, Freemasonry was part of their cultural baggage. The appeal of Freemasonry in England, and its swift spread across the European continent, appears to stem from the harmony between the Masonic ideals of honesty and integrity and the newer currents of religious and political thought. The settlers were coming out of Britain at a time when the power of the autocratic government and absolutist church was eroding. The settlers, often those most firmly insistent upon the need for change, derived intellectual sustenance from the Masonic principles. That English Freemasonry was imitated in the colonies is not surprising for it connoted social prestige. Freemasonry in England was sponsored early by the nobility, and the prestigious appeal to the merchant, professional, and literary classes followed in course. Religious toleration, belief in liberty, personal and civic morality, equality and peace—all were beliefs of the newly developing middle class.[1] These were compatible with the prestige of power surrounding all England touched in the early eighteenth century.[2]

Masonic membership indicated that a man was free-thinking and philanthropic; membership was also a sign of respectability. Masonry was more suspect on the Continent. Pope Clement

1. Frank A. Hankins, "Masonry," *Encyclopedia of the Social Sciences,* vol. 10; J. M. Roberts, *The Mythology of the Secret Societies.* See also David Hawke, *The Colonial Experience,* for a discussion of the temper of the times. What little protest emerged concerning English Freemasonry centered around the immorality assumed, not the revolutionary potential.

2. See Winthrop Jordan, *White Over Black: American Attitudes Toward the Negro, 1550–1812,* for an excellent discussion of the nature and extent of American Anglophilia. Roberts, *Mythology,* p. 28, suggests *Anglomania* as a term encompassing the prevalence of faddishness and admiration of anything English.

XII's Papal Bull in 1738 against Freemasonry, labeled as invidious, is one indication of the threat felt by churches and monarchs.[3]

Within the American colonies during the 1730s, Freemasons became visible as groups with influence in the leading cities. Many of the colonists had been initiated into the brotherhood earlier in England and France. Discussing the awakening of American nationalistic feelings, Carl Degler asserted that the spread of Freemasonry accelerated communication within and between the colonies. Degler stated that Masonic lodges were well established by 1741 and that those Masons who traveled in the service of Freemasonry served to bring together those who might not otherwise have met.

It must be remembered that Americans, in general, did not constitute a community or nation as such in the latter part of the eighteenth century. Individuals and communities were isolated, and little was known outside the familiar grouping other than secondhand information or rumor brought in by travelers, who were often viewed as exotic. Historical records indicate that some of these persons were Masons, and thus more quickly accepted as honest and forthright men of note.[4]

Freemasonry reflected the values of the fledgling colonies and nation. To its adherents it offered mystery, a sense of brotherhood, the excitement of mystical ceremonies, and the symbolic maintenance of a tie with the mother country. Initially a grouping of the most powerful persons in the colonies, it became a potential mobility channel for those desiring such position or status.[5] Since George Washington, General Lafayette, Benjamin Franklin, and other leaders of the colonies were Masons, it was also a drawing card for new converts.

The Masonic way embodies gentility, a code of values and manners reflecting a higher inner quality. This genteel aura created an appealing lure for the colonial upwardly mobile, the more status conscious of the new American breed of commu-

3. Norman MacKenzie, *Secret Societies,* chapter seven.
4. Carl N. Degler, *Out of the Past: The Forces That Shaped Modern America.*
5. The first colonial Mason is said to have been Jonathan Belcher, governor of the Massachusetts Bay Colony, who had been made a Mason in England in 1704. For greater detail, see Henry C. Coil, W. R. Hervery, and Charles C. Hunt, "Masonic Fraternity," *Encyclopedia Americana,* pp. 383–89b. St. John's Lodge at Boston was the first official lodge in the colonies.

nity leaders. Secondly, the Masonic order was an ideal hedge for those increasingly aware of their ambivalence over no longer being true Englishmen, but men having a unique set of problems and perhaps even values.[6] Thirdly, the Masonic way of life bridged the gap between acceptance of religious tolerance as a vital part of a republican doctrine and the reality of the declining significance of religion. In the early eighteenth century, it has been argued, there were more "un-churched people" living in America than in any other Western country.[7] Not only was religion on the decline because of Enlightenment ideas, but formal church attendance was becoming more frequently interrupted as the Revolutionary War approached.

By the time of the American Revolution, there were approximately one hundred settled lodges in particular communities and fifty military lodges. Prominent persons in American history belonged to these lodges. Numerous Masons were among the signers of the Declaration of Independence and the members of the Constitutional Convention.[8] There was soon a matter for white Masons to contend with: an organization structurally and ideologically identical with the mainstream body but racially different in membership. It emerged from the situation encountered by a small number of free blacks who were integrally involved in the general prerevolutionary fervor of the 1770s.

In 1775, a young twenty-seven-year-old black man named Prince Hall addressed the Massachusetts Committee of Safety. A leader in the black community, Hall urged the enlistment of both slaves and freedmen into the movement to free the colonies from inhumane British control. Hall was concerned with the rightful development of the colonies; he was also convinced that the involvement of black persons would be the first step

6. See Jordan, *White Over Black,* part four, for a thorough discussion of the difficulties the colonists and revolutionists had in working out national identities separate from England. Jack P. Greene, "Search for Identity: An Interpretation of the Meaning of Selected Patterns of Social Response in Eighteenth-Century America," *Journal of Social History,* pp. 189–220, also discusses the conflicting tensions resulting from an overidealized image of both English patterns of behavior and the early colonial past.

7. Hawke, *The Colonial Experience;* Greene, "Search for Identity."

8. Georg Simmel, "The Secret and the Secret Society," in *The Sociology of Georg Simmel,* ed. and trans. Kurt H. Wolff, p. 348.

toward the complete freedom of the slaves. The Massachusetts Committee of Safety, with John Hancock and Joseph Warren as members, declined the suggestion.[9]

In the buildup of revolutionary fervor, Prince Hall, prominent in the Boston community for his activities directed toward the betterment of the community, joined others identifying freedom for the colonists with freedom for the black slave.[10] Boston was the center of colonial discontent at this time. Bernard Bailyn contended that the colonists saw their struggle as political, constitutional, and ideological. Based on a "radical idealization and conceptualization" of the immediate past, efforts were originally reformist; rebellion for a separate state was not of initial concern. The question of the extent and character of England's jurisdiction over the colonies involved a wide range of social and political problems that became conceptualized into the special and chosen nature of the American people. As Bailyn expressed it: ". . . Americans had come to think of themselves as in a special category uniquely placed by history to capitalize on, to complete and fulfill, the promise of man's existence."[11]

Some joined attacks on slavery as an institution with other human rights concerns. The parallel between the colonists' lack of control over their destiny and the state of powerlessness of a chattel slave was cited. Newssheets and pamphlets highlighted the contrast between what political leaders in the colonies were espousing for themselves and what was actually imposed or tolerated by others. A small measure of support grew for the conjoined freedom of the colonists with freedom of the black slave. Free blacks such as Prince Hall had reason to feel the

9. Harry E. Davis, *A History of Freemasonry Among Negroes in America*, p. 14; Harold Van Buren Voorhis, *Negro Masonry in the United States*, p. 24.

10. See Bernard Bailyn, *The Ideological Origins of the American Revolution*, chapter six for examples from speeches and articles of this period. Winthrop Jordan, *White Over Black*, also presents a thorough discussion of the Revolution era in part three and substantiates the mood of the period as being conducive to hopefulness. His major focus is on the attitudes of white settlers; however, it can easily be inferred that this process had a marked effect on the thought-patternings of the free blacks. See also Lerone Bennett, Jr., "Pioneers in Protest: Prince Hall," *Ebony*, p. 89.

11. Bailyn, *Ideological Origins*, p. 20. Their psychological break with English society and culture was far from complete, however. See Greene, "Search for Identity," on this point.

contradiction between the espousal of revolutionary philosophies and the realities of the colonies would lead to movement on the part of the nation's leaders to change the degraded status of all blacks, slave and free. Prince Hall and others protested and petitioned, utilizing ideas and techniques of the colonists' struggle with Britain. It is in this context, and out of a belief in the integrity of the Masonic brotherhood, that Prince Hall and fourteen other free black men petitioned for admittance to the white Boston St. John's Lodge, the first Masonic lodge officially authorized by the Mother Lodge of England.[12]

This petition was not the first attempt by blacks to join a Masonic organization. Some whites were outraged in the 1730s at the "impudence" of some blacks assuming the "stile and title of Free Masons, in Imitation of a Society here . . . a Gross Affront to the Provincial Grand Master and Gentlemen of the Fraternity."[13] There is no record of black action following the rebuff, nor a similar outraged statement in the Boston community: the men were turned away.

Thus, prior to the Revolutionary War, a lodge within the British forces based in Boston came forward to welcome these black individuals as Masonic brethren. The initiation into Freemasonry in 1775 of fifteen blacks by an Irish regiment in the British forces—Lodge No. 441, Irish Registry, attached to the 38th Foot Regiment anchored in Boston harbor—is the seed of the long tradition of Masonic affiliation of blacks in the United States.[14]

The British Army was the catalyst, witting or unwitting, for a broader change in the American black experience. A proclamation by Lord Dunmore assured blacks that if they enlisted in the British forces they would be granted freedom at the end of the

12. The status of first is disputed by the New Jersey Provincial Grand Lodge (mainstream). However, consensus seems to show that the New Jersey body did not act on their warrant until after St. John's Lodge was in existence.

13. Jordan, *White Over Black,* p. 130. See also Bennett, "Pioneers in Protest," p. 51; William Grimshaw, *Official History of Freemasonry Among the Colored People in North America,* p. 42.

14. Charles H. Wesley, *Prince Hall: Life and Legacy,* p. 4. The Irish were the most revolutionary elements in the British population at this time. See Robert Blauner, "Marxian Theory and Race Relations," paper presented at the 1972 meetings of the American Sociological Association, for parallels between Irish nationalism and contemporary American civil rights.

war.[15] It was only after the British forces were using blacks as troops that the Continental Army saw fit to change its adamant refusal to officially endorse blacks as soldiers.[16] The facts suggest that black acceptance by the military did not come about for moral reasons or because of the intrinsic worth of the black man. Neither was the need for manpower the major determining factor. On the part of the Continental forces, it was a pragmatic assessment that blacks could better be used fighting against the British. Approximately five thousand blacks came to fight for the colonies. A larger number served with the British, who left the American shores with almost four times as many African-Americans as those supporting the revolutionary forces.[17]

It may be that motivation of the British Masons to admit black seekers was a political strategy to ensure black commitment to the British cause. This is doubtful given that Prince Hall and others had openly expressed their views in support of the validity of the colonists' complaints against the British. One Masonic historian, Harry A. Williamson, Prince Hall affiliation, wrote in 1924:

> The motive of the English Masonic officers in initiating these 15 colored men into the Masonic fraternity has been, and I suppose will always be a mystery. Whether it was for cooperation by Negroes they hoped to get against the colonies; or if it might be an exercise of "Brotherly Love for the whole human species as one family," I suppose we will never know.[18]

At this time the military forces were merely a regulatory body to enforce Parliament's legislation of the colonies, which makes it more likely, as other Masonic historians maintain, that the army lodge's action was a genuine manifestation of one of the solemn obligations assumed by members: the spreading of the Masonic light worldwide. The initiation procedure, called the "making"

15. Among those slaves who did accept the offer were many from the plantation of Thomas Jefferson. See Bennett, "Pioneers in Protest," p. 89, for a discussion of this point.

16. James E. Blackwell, *The Black Community: Diversity and Unity*, p. 219.

17. Bennett, "Pioneers in Protest," p. 51. See also the excellent treatment of the British government's subsequent handling of these individuals in Mary Beth Norton, "The Fate of Some Black Loyalists of the American Revolution," *The Journal of Negro History*, pp. 402–26.

18. *National Fraternal Review*, 24 May 1924, p. 3.

of Masons, was a common practice for military lodges under English, Irish, and Scottish Masonic constitutions.[19]

It is logical to assume that the free black men of Boston saw a ray of hope for justice in the Masonic philosophy of uplift of the human race and in the revolutionary protestations, with their blending of humanitarianism and natural and equal rights philosophies.[20] It is in this context that Prince Hall and other free blacks were initiated into Freemasonry. But, given the nature and course of the colonial rebellion, their settled place within white Freemasonry was short-lived. After the Irish lodge left the area, Prince Hall and his fellow Masons were left with limited powers. They could not confer Masonic degrees. Prince Hall applied unsuccessfully to mainstream provincial Masonic authorities for a temporary full warrant while they waited to hear from the headquarters of Freemasonry in England. He did receive, however, a second permit to continue "the work of the craft"[21] from John Rowe, provisional grant master, that covered the period until the necessary charter could be obtained for a separate lodge from the Grand Lodge of England.[22] The first meeting place for the black Masons was a lodge room they prepared in "Golden Fleece," which was located on Water Street near the Boston harbor. They later met at Kirby Street Temple in Boston.[23]

Soon, the grand master of the Mother Grand Lodge of England, H. R. H. The Duke of Cumberland, supported the Irish regiment's earlier actions by issuing a charter for the separate functioning of African Lodge No. 459.[24] The Prince Hall Ma-

19. Some European, Australian, and West Indian lodges initiated blacks into their groups. The early Philadelphia Prince Hall roster for 1797 through 1808 shows thirty-two men as having been made Masons while in Europe and the West Indies. The early records of the Washington, D. C., black lodges show seven such members. See Harry E. Davis, "Documents Relating to Negro Masonry in America," *Journal of Negro History*, p. 166.
20. See Wesley, *Prince Hall*, chapter three; Greene, "Search for Identity."
21. The term *work* in the Masonic framework refers to the ritualistic procedures of operation of the ideological and meeting procedures. See Grimshaw, *Official History*, p. 67.
22. Davis, *History of Freemasonry*.
23. Grimshaw, *Official History*, p. 72.
24. The Mother Lodge's recognition of the validity of the action by the Irish regiment is important given the controversy over the legitimacy of black Freemasonry. The usual Masonic practice was for no more than one lodge to exist in a particular geographical area. Some, with hindsight, have

sons experience much satisfaction from being able to loudly proclaim that they are the only body of black men in America able to date and document their existence as an organized body from 1775 to the present.[25] The charter, dated 29 September 1784, was personally delivered to Prince Hall by James Scott, a sea captain and brother-in-law of the eminent John Hancock. The charter now rests intact in a vault in a Boston bank. It is the only original charter held by any American Masonic body. It was granted firsthand by the Mother Grand Lodge of England and has been an item of particular veneration and worth to the membership. When a fire destroyed the original grand lodge meeting place, priceless records were lost. The charter, however, was then kept in a metal tube in a chest. It is said that William B. Kendall, a past grand master, crawled into the burning building to save the charter. Another story is told of the charter being hidden in an old elm tree on the Boston Commons for four years when the Boston Prince Hall Masons felt that it might be stolen by white Masons who have, at various times, offered a considerable sum of money for the document.

Prince Hall Freemasonry, so designated after the death of the first black Masonic leader in 1807, spread rapidly.[26] Exalted by

disputed the Irish lodge's jurisdiction in making these gentlemen, or any other gentleman, Masons. One argument is that the provisional grand lodge of the Bay Colony had explicitly acted to bar the military lodge from such actions in the early 1770s. See Harvey N. Brown, *Freemasonry Among Negroes and Whites in America,* p. 20. It is argued elsewhere that the Bay Colony lodge was itself Masonically irregular and thus in no position to bar others' Masonic activities. See Lewis Hayden, "Masonry Among Colored Men in Massachusetts," p. 30. Other versions of this dispute will be discussed later.

25. This, for example, is one of the main points in "Historical Sketch," a speech written by Grand Historian Cleo W. Wooten, Massachusetts grand lodge, delivered initially on 24 June 1951. Evidence of particular pride on this point can be found in the literature (see, for example, Brown, *Freemasonry Among Negroes,* and interview data).

26. Prince Hall died from pneumonia alledgedly contracted while going to the aid of a fellow Mason in distress. An impressive Masonic funeral service was conducted. The burial at Copp's Hill Durying Ground, a prestigious cemetery, was attended by both black and white Masons, an interesting fact in light of the controversy to come, even though the white Masons attended the service as autonomous individuals. See Voorhis, *Negro Masonry,* chapter one, for a further discussion of this event. Each year the Massachusetts grand lodge makes a visit to Prince Hall's grave for a solemn commemoration service. Hall's successor, said by one writer to be of

black Masons as a "spiritual radical,"[27] Prince Hall is clearly pivotal to the emergence of African Lodge No. 459 and to the evolution of black Freemasonry. He has assumed mythical stature over the years but some factual details can be discerned. Most historians note that he was born in the West Indies and came to the Boston colony in 1765 from Bridgetown, Barbados, in search of a more challenging life. Hall's father is said to have been an English leather merchant, his mother a free black of French descent.[28] Hall had been apprenticed to his father, but seeing little chance for advancement he obtained a working passage to the colonies when he was seventeen years old. At the time of his arrival the situation for free blacks in the colony was deteriorating at an accelerating speed. The rate of unemployment was higher for free blacks than the comparable figure for current black unemployment in the United States.[29] Hall worked and studied and became increasingly appalled at the socioeconomic conditions of blacks and the indifference of white patriots to this situation.

In 1766, Boston blacks filed a petition against slavery, receiving support for this organized effort from various outlying areas as far as the Connecticut colonies. Meetings were held to develop a larger unified body that could exert concerted pressure, and some private manumissions did occur that can be traced to this effort. It is likely that Hall was involved with these meetings. In any event, one finds Hall on the rolls of the colony in 1773 as a property holder, taxpayer, and voter.

At the time of the emergence of Prince Hall as a leader in Boston there was a large proportion of free blacks in the popula-

---

Russian-Jewish extraction, led the group for two years until he was called to Russia to fight in the Napoleonic wars. See Davis, *History of Freemasonry*, p. 192.

27. Davis, *History of Freemasonry*, p. 41.

28. Davis, *History of Freemasonry*, p. 411; Grimshaw, *Official History*, pp. 75–83; Voorhis, *Negro Masonry*. The eminent historian, Charles Wesley, has recently evaluated the legends concerning Prince Hall and now holds that there is insufficient evidence concerning his place of birth and his parentage. Brown, *Freemasonry Among Negroes*, contends that Hall was a slave for twenty-one years in the Massachusetts colony attached to the family of an American leather merchant. See also Donn A. Cass, *Negro Freemasonry and Segregation*, p. 11.

29. See Edgar M. McManus, *Black Bondage in the North*, p. 71; Randall Butts, "A New School Named 'Prince Hall,' " p. 8.

tion. The free blacks had a status midway between slave and citizen. While opportunities for social mobility were blocked, as were residential areas, they remained subject to taxation in similar manner to other residents. The times when citizen status was recognized were those when it cound benefit the white population.

A large body of repressive racial legislation existed in the New England colonies. In Connecticut, blacks had to be off the streets by 9:00 P.M. whether free or slave, and had to remain in their own areas. Flogging was a punishment there and in Massachusetts for curfew violations. Free blacks, Indians, indentured servants, and slaves had to abide by the restrictions imposed by the slave codes: boundaries beyond which they could not travel, curfew of 9:00 P.M., nonuse of ferries, no entertainment of Indians or black slaves in free black homes, nonparticipation in the militia, and so forth. Codified regulation resulted from the increasing number of slaves in New England. During the period from 1756 to 1774 the proportion of slaves to free inhabitants increased; in Connecticut, for example, there was a forty percent increase.[30]

In 1774, after being influenced by the outdoor preachers on the Boston Commons, Hall was converted to Methodism, and, after five years of study, appears to have become a clergyman or lay official of a church in the Cambridge area.[31] He is mentioned by contemporary Masons as having seen the "spiritual depression" of the free blacks and having moved to meet this need.[32] Hall was outspoken on the inconsistencies of the patriots between their principles and actions. His was a conscious decision to use legal processes to fight for the rights of all blacks, and he preached to blacks the virtue of solidarity and collective action. To the powers that controlled the colonies he stressed the words and assumptions of the revolutionary doctrines. A slight, light-complexioned man, he is said to have been perceived by white politicians as an exceptional member of the black race.[33]

---

30. See McManus, *Black Bondage*, chapter five, for an extensive discussion of these practices. See also Lorenzo J. Greene, "Prince Hall: Massachusetts Leader in Crisis," *Freedomways*.

31. See Wesley, *Prince Hall*, p. 22, for a discussion of the evidence.

32. See, for example, Grimshaw, *Official History*, p. 70.

33. Some chose to trace his eruditeness to his white blood. See Bennett, "Pioneers in Protest," on this point.

The early hopefulness of free blacks with the rise of revolutionary fervor was soon dashed, however, as various steps were taken after the Revolution to legislate all blacks into an "ever-shrinking corner of the American community."[34] At the end of the Revolutionary War, the black population was twenty percent of the total population. Eight percent of these were free blacks.[35]

An organized body of "free men of color" was an anomaly in a system reaping the benefits of both the slave trade and the slave labor system. As Winthrop Jordan succinctly expressed it: "The association of slavery with race had transformed a free black man into a walking contradiction in terms, a social anomaly, a third party in a system built for two."[36]

34. See Jordan, *White Over Black*, p. 403, for further discussion of this point.

35. Bennett, "The Black Pioneer Period," *Ebony*, pp. 46–55.

36. Jordan, *White Over Black*, p. 134. Compare Booker T. Washington, *The Story of the Negro: The Rise of the Race from Slavery*, p. 193; Ira Berlin, *Slaves Without Masters: The Free Negro in the Antebellum South.*

Chapter 3

The Free Black Context

The foundation for the institutional infrastructure of the black community was firmly entrenched by the latter quarter of the eighteenth century. The experience of free blacks in the colonies and the new nation played a major role in its formation. In a detailed social history of the free black experience in the South from the emergence of the new nation through 1812 and in the decade of the 1850s, Ira Berlin demonstrated that the free blacks were an anomalous caste in a system built for two.[1] Throughout the entire country, free blacks drew an inordinate but particular amount of attention from the general society, and civil authorities pondered means to contain the development and function of a strong black community.

Before the Revolutionary War, free blacks were typically the offspring of interracial unions, usually those between white indentured servants and black slaves. As difficulties with the British increasingly preoccupied the settlers, individual slaveowners selectively freed individual slaves, further increasing the small free black population. The more liberal manumission practices, though small in number, combined with an increased number of successful escapes from slavery to produce an expansion of the free black population. As the number of freed blacks mushroomed, statutes and policies circumscribing their rights became increasingly codified.

The development of an urban base, with its potential for greater collective protest and affirmation of efforts, was clearly perceived by white leaders as a threat. Larger numbers of individual blacks were migrating to southern and northern cities since these centers offered protection of a sort and a relatively greater measure of autonomy existed in these settings. There were more job opportunities and, due to close quarters, others to help in times of need. Discrimination in housing practices led to

1. Ira Berlin's *Slaves Without Masters: The Free Negro in the Antebellum South* has proved invaluable to this study.

21

dense black settlements, often around wharves and alleys. From this mix emerged a small number of urban artisans, skilled craftsmen, and small businessmen who earned their living from the white economy.[2]

The parameters surrounding the degree of *freeness* of the free blacks, however, were marked:

> The free Negro was known as "free", but in none of these states was he as free as the white man. He was, however, a part of the community. It was possible that there were those who exercised political rights but even in the free states the property and special qualifications were barriers to a general participation by free Negroes in the exercise of the suffrage.[3]

The free black's place in the evolving social system was insecure. Whereas the black slave had a place in the structure, albeit a negative one, the free black had no permanent place within either the white or the traditional black system in the eyes of the white settlers, even though blacks in both instances were necessary factors for the function of the society and the development of the economy. "Just as slavery allegedly freed southern whites for the leisurely pursuit of culture, so did the free Negro worker enable northern whites to engage in more vital activities . . . Negroes performed a psychological service in that their work allowed whites to assume aristocratic airs . . ."[4] Antagonism from white laborers, however, had a major part in the problems of free blacks.[5] In 1830, for example, the president of a trade union in Cincinnati was publicly tried for apprenticing a black youth. In that town, ostensibly in the North, black and white children were not allowed to play together because of the rigid

2. By 1850, New York City alone recorded free blacks in fourteen trades. A number were wealthy caterers and barbers; Martin E. Dann, *The Black Press, 1827–1890: The Quest for National Identity*. The New York City Chamber of Commerce was founded in a black owned restaurant in New York City. See Lerone Bennett, Jr., "The Black Pioneer Period," *Ebony*, pp. 46–55.

3. Charles H. Wesley, *Neglected History: Essays in Negro American History by a College President*, p. 44.

4. Leon F. Litwack, *North of Slavery: The Negro in the Free States, 1790–1860*, pp. 156–57.

5. For a thorough discussion of labor antagonism, see William J. Wilson, *The Declining Significance of Race*. See also Edgar J. McManus, *Black Bondage in the North*.

ostracism stemming from the intensity of the competition over labor.[6]

The number of free blacks in urban centers was indeed sizable. In 1837 there were approximately 320,000 free blacks in such areas, with 44,000 persons estimated in the State of New York alone; 22,000 in the New England states; 18,000 in New Jersey; 38,000 in Pennsylvania; and 200,000 distributed throughout the other states. The 1850 census shows that there were well-established free black communities in many of the border states, with clusterings around Baltimore (25, 442 free blacks), Washington (8,158), Charleston (3,441), and New Orleans (9,905).[7]

These free blacks established and strengthened the infrastructure of the black community: churches, benevolent societies, and fraternal groups were the core of the free black community. Circumstances led blacks, subject to castelike restrictions, to depend strongly upon each other. This does not imply, however, that the free black caste was homogeneous. There was much diversity within the group, but there was also a general cohesiveness important for survival. The social-status system within the black caste developed during slavery and was reinforced by the urban context. Among the criteria used for internal stratification purposes were free or slave background, occupation, shade of skin color, prominence of one's employer or mentor, and degree of civic virtue.[8]

Berlin makes a most persuasive case for the impact of the differing experience of free blacks in the Upper and Lower South. In the Upper South, whites tended to characterize slavery as a necessary evil for American society, whereas whites in the Lower South thought of slavery as a positive good. These differing perceptions had an impact upon the black experience and upon white perception of the disruptive potential of free blacks. In the Lower South whites hoped that the urban free black community would erode away, but there was not a large enough number of free blacks remaining in the South, other than easily absorbable or isolated Creoles, to be perceived as a genuine threat. In the Upper South, however, the number and

6. See Wendell P. Dabney, *Cincinnati's Colored Citizens,* pp. 34–36.
7. Berlin, *Slaves Without Masters;* Dann, *The Black Press.*
8. August Meier and Elliott Rudwick, *From Plantation to Ghetto.*

physical appearance of free blacks, more often rural than urban, was closer to that of the chattel slaves. This similarity was a source of anxiety for slaveowners who feared that free blacks would agitate and negatively influence their slaves.

The realities for blacks in the seventeenth and eighteenth centuries, in the North and in both regions of the South, did have many similarities. For example, New England in colonial times was a participant in the slave trade, although participation was in a relatively selective manner. Interestingly, more women and children coming directly from Africa were brought into the New England colonies than other areas.[9] Slave trading itself was important for New England's commercial prosperity. Massachusetts had the highest financial investment in slave trading, with Rhode Island second. It was the money accumulated from selling slaves in the South, for the most part, that generated the capital to stimulate the growth of New England industries.[10] This had an effect on the general manner in which all blacks in that area were treated. In the North, though full participation and rights were lacking, the colonies at various times granted some degree of legal rights and relative justice for blacks. However, as the colonists began to be alarmed about the failure to immediately attain an unproblematic life of plenty in the new country, restrictions began to emerge. Beginning in the 1680s, the Massachusetts colony defined and restricted black movement and behavior through a myriad of evolving laws.[11]

Initially, a number of free blacks lived on scraps of land that no one else wanted out in the country away from the main roadways. Those who had been freed from completion of their period of indentured servitude in the very first decades of slave trading—a small number at best—quietly tended plots of land that had been given to them or that they had purchased. In the South, in particular, this was often prime land. Still others lived near their white employers, in some cases being quartered with

9. Lorenzo Greene, *The Negro in Colonial New England*, pp. 36–37.

10. See Greene, *Colonial New England*, and McManus, *Black Bondage*, regarding this period. In 1763, the Massachusetts slave trade employed about 5,000 sailors as well as persons who serviced the ships. No stigma was attached to being the owner of, or working on, these ships.

11. Robert C. Twombly and Robert H. Moore, "Black Puritan: The Negro in Seventeenth-Century Massachusetts," *William & Mary Quarterly*, p. 238.

the slaves.[12] Regional differences can also be seen in the relative degrees of *freeness* for the free black. For example, in the Gulf region, settled by the French and Spanish, the free black population typically stemmed from the light-complexioned progeny of white settlers mating with black women. In some areas, such as Louisiana, free blacks had a relatively higher status than free blacks in the colonies settled by the English.[13] Their problems were less stressful legally, but social discrimination and barriers to full equality did exist, sometimes in petty form. Berlin cites evidence that "Spanish officials even regulated the dress of free Negro women to assure whites a monopoly of frills and feathers."[14]

It was pragmatic for free and newly freed blacks to attempt to carry themselves as differently as possible from those still enslaved. It was necessary that the community be able to delineate the characteristics of virtue and respect of the freed black man or woman. While sympathies remained with the oppressed masses, the free blacks had their own lives and interests to protect.

Shade of skin color was often an important infragroup distinction:

> During the colonial era, most Negro freedmen vowed their liberty to their "white blood" and some had benefitted from close relations with whites. The appearance of a large number of free blacks, as opposed to mulattoes, may have intensified the free Negro's consciousness of color.[15]

Divisions, however, were relatively flexible. Marriage often crossed the lines, as did religious practices and use of leisure time. "Friendships sparked in the workshops, churches, and groceries where free Negroes and slaves rubbed elbows reinforced race loyalties and encouraged free Negroes to help slaves to freedom with forged passes, with loans of money, or simply by standing as their masters."[16] However, free blacks knew that

12. See Berlin, *Slaves Without Masters,* chapter eight, for a thorough discussion of the beginnings of communities of free blacks.

13. See Winthrop Jordan, *White Over Black: American Attitudes Toward the Black, 1550–1010,* and Berlin, *Slaves Without Masters,* for a discussion of the cultural traditions regarding treatment of slaves by Anglo, French, and Spanish settlers.

14. Berlin, *Slaves Without Masters,* p. 110.

15. Ibid., p. 57.

16. Ibid., p. 270.

practicality defined their life situations and chances, and that pragmatically they could not act as militant revolutionists attempting to free the enslaved population. As Berlin states it:

> Thus the central paradox of free Negro life was that while full equality depended on the unity of all blacks, free and slave, and the abolition of slavery, substantial gains could more realistically be obtained within the existing society by standing apart from the slaves. Consciously or unconsciously, upward-striving free Negroes understood this and acted on it.[17]

An estimated eight percent of the black population was counted as free in the first census taken in 1790. The census report noted that "exclusive organizations, based on color, economic status and high moral standards, had begun to take form" among blacks.[18] These organizations were functionally important for the maintenance of a status midway between slave and full citizen. The exclusivity, and the particular defensiveness concerning it, has often been treated as mere pretention. Pressures converging on skilled free blacks, however, made the emergence of these organizations inevitable.[19]

> The southern free Negroes who had some property in the days of slavery had to be very tightly exclusive to preserve their small advantages. One runaway slave caught in their midst would have threatened the whole group; it was best to admit no new people to their churches and no outsiders to the cemeteries that were the symbol of their independence.[20]

In the South, too, economic success was intricately entwined with the utilization of slave labor. Some free blacks in the South were themselves slaveowners: "Although most free Negro slaveholders were truly benevolent despots, owning only their families and friends to prevent their enslavement or forcible deportation, a small minority of wealthy freemen exploited slaves for commercial purposes. This small group of free Negroes were generally the wealthiest and best-connected mem-

17. Ibid., p. 271.

18. E. Horace Fitchett, "The Origin and Growth of the Free Negro Population of Charleston, South Carolina," *Journal of Negro History*, p. 434.

19. Edna Bonacich suggests that the defensiveness of a middleman minority is a universal. See "A Theory of Middleman Minorities," *American Sociological Review*, pp. 583– 94.

20. Everett C. Hughes and Helen M. Hughes, *Where People Meet: Racial and Ethnic Frontiers*, p. 110.

bers of their caste."[21] It is this latter group, the beginning of the black *upper* class, rather than the black middle class that tended to strive for identity with the white upper class. It is this group, small in number, that is mistakenly considered to be the black middle class, described in the sociological literature as having a flair for conspicuous high living.

The numerical extent, and sociological import, of this segment of the population should not be exaggerated, for the wealthy free black knew well how his money had been earned and how the wider society actually operated.

> Having climbed to the top of free Negro society, the elite could see, perhaps as poorer freemen could not, the full extent of the world that whites kept from them. Many successful free Negroes despised the lucrative but demeaning service trades that provided the economic basis of their elevated positions. They yearned to be teachers, lawyers, doctors, while whites forced them to work as barbers and barmen. "I hate the name barber," one successful Alabama free Negro told his son, "there are so many superior occupations." Although elite free Negroes served cheerfully and acquiesced to "their place" in Southern society with hardly a murmur, they never forgave whites.[22]

Antagonisms continued to exist between those blacks without such skills and those with skills of the same nature as whites. A regional dimension was added to this antagonism as the northern-born freedman was more likely to have developed skills than the newly emancipated Southerner. A response by some latter black persons was to view the northern freedmen as pretentious, further fuel for the impression of black exclusivity as a pretentious ornament rather than a functional protection.

In social situations, then, free blacks of varying interests and occupations sought to demonstrate, both to themselves and to their clients and neighbors, their fitness as equal social beings. The method many chose was fraternal organizations, with the leading one being Freemasonry.

21. Berlin, *Slaves Without Masters,* p. 273.
22. Ibid., p. 280.

Chapter 4

Nineteenth-Century
Realities for Free Blacks

In the eighteenth and nineteenth centuries, there were many industrious black artisans, some highly skilled, in the North. There were bakers, barbers, blacksmiths, carpenters, cabinet-makers, caterers, coopers, fishermen, mechanics, printers, sailmakers, shipwrights, tailors, weavers, and so forth. In several of these areas, barbering for one, blacks had a monopoly on the market. Yet in 1800 there were still 36,505 northern blacks still in bondage.[1]

In the latter part of the eighteenth century, following events such as Shays's Rebellion, the French Revolution, and the Haitian Revolution, expectations arose throughout the black population. Whereas blacks saw a hope for change, many whites felt their sense of group position and advantage threatened and a conservative reaction became entrenched. New legislative and judicial restrictions upon persons of color emerged multifold. A repressive period followed in which blacks were randomly assaulted, in some cases burned, and generally barred from public activities. The wartime years of common cause yielded to an increase in conservatism as evidenced in the drafting of state and federal constitutions. The Constitution gave permission for fifteen more years of importation of slaves, and a decision was made to allow southern states to base their representation on a population including slaves. This sealed off revolutionary hopes for black freedom.[2]

It was in this period, in 1787, that Richard Allen and Absolum Jones walked out of the white church that they had previously

1. Leon F. Litwack, *North of Slavery: The Negro in the Free States, 1790–1860;* Edgar J. McManus, *Black Bondage in the North.* Both present a thorough analysis of the complexity of the northern slave regime, its diversification, and its impact on status rankings.
2. A most thorough account of this period can be found in Ira Berlin, *Slaves Without Masters: The Free Negro in the Antebellum South,* chapter three.

been attending to protest against the new segregationist policies regarding seating that were being instituted in white churches. The Free African Society was formed as a religious and mutual aid body. It became the first black Episcopal church.

By the War of 1812 there had developed a proliferation of black churches of various denominations.[3] Ira Berlin, studying the emergence of the various black churches, noted that "although the rank discrimination of the white-dominated church fostered black separatism, clearly many blacks welcomed the split." The blacks, often more numerous than whites within the parish church, finally had a degree of control over their religious practices.[4] This level of control, albeit over only a small domain of their life's conditions, appears to have been generative of esteem for both the group and the self.

Various problems arose for free blacks after the Revolutionary War from the diverse number of conflicting statutes that emerged: "The federal government and the individual states separately defined the legal status of antebellum free Negroes. Prior to the Fourteenth and Fifteenth amendments, each state determined their political and educational rights."[5] The autonomy of the individual states led to a number of repressive measures as the number of free blacks increased. During a twenty-year period from 1790 to 1810, the proportion of free blacks rose from eight percent of the total black population to more than thirteen percent. Various legislative statutes attest to the sharpening mood to restrict black movement. In North Carolina a 1785 measure called for a cloth badge with the word *free* upon it to be physically displayed on the clothing of such blacks at all times. Georgia specified that free blacks were subject to the slave laws.

---

3. Lerone Bennett, Jr., has argued that the black church is another example of the direct intervention of British action on American soil. He claims that the first black churches, albeit single organizations that did not spread, were in Williamsburg, Virginia, and Augusta, Georgia, in 1776. Both were founded by servants of British officers who were left behind. Thus, the Allen and Jones church is the first large-scale, rather than the first ever, and is the first leading to a major denomination. See Berlin, *Slaves Without Masters,* chapter two, for the vicissitudes concerning religious practices and profession of blacks.

4. Berlin, *Slaves Without Masters,* p. 71.

5. Leon F. Litwack, "The Federal Government and the Free Negro, 1790–1860," *Journal of Negro History,* p. 261.

Various other states enacted such discriminatory measures as taxes, unusual licensing requirements, or restrictions. In Virginia urban free blacks had to register with the town clerk listing not only age, sex, and occupation but also all "identifying marks, and how they were freed." They were not only required to register but to pay for the process of registration itself. The rural free blacks were given more freedom: they were required to do this only once every three years instead of once a year as required of free urban blacks. Maryland and Tennessee adopted similar procedures.

News traveled quickly of an alleged increased number of slave escapes or uprisings.[6] Maryland accused free blacks of inciting the slaves to steal produce from their masters to give to the free black population. A 1796 prohibition on the sale of agricultural produce by free blacks emerged as a result. In Georgia and Virginia, licenses for free black river captains and pilots were not renewed, "thus barring them from a lucrative and prestigious aspect of a trade that blacks dominated."[7]

A resolution of the Maryland legislature in 1831 evidenced the growing fear of black progress:

> Resolved, that the increased proportion of the free people of color, in this State, to the white population—the evils growing out of their connection and unrestrained association with the slaves, their habits and manner of obtaining a subsistence, and their withdrawing a large portion of employment from the laboring class of the white population, are subjects of momentum and grave consideration.

Cited in defense of this resolution was the practice in Georgia of fining whites five hundred dollars for teaching free blacks to read and write; also cited was the practice of whippings for black preachers. South Carolina established a prohibition against the assembly of free blacks, even when whites were present. Such a meeting, "in a confined or secret place, for the purpose of mental instruction, is an unlawful assembly," punishable by dispersal and whipping.[8] Free blacks were, in general, subject to random extralegal terrorism, vigilante style. This was an integral part of the control system since legal methods of enforcing registration, licensing, travel restrictions, and so forth, had

6. Bennett, "Pioneers in Protest: Prince Hall," *Ebony,* pp. 46–55.
7. Berlin, *Slaves Without Masters,* pp. 92–97.
8. Linda Warfel Slaughter, *Freedmen of the South.*

proved or were proving cumbersome and slow.[9] Whether these practices and a multitude of statutes were consistently enforced is not the issue; their existence and sporadic enforcement is sufficient to indicate the mood of the times and the control of the white power structure.

The North-South antagonism of this time must also be noted. The North had trained its blacks, free and slave, to meet the needs of its diverse economy. During the debate over statehood for slave states, Southerners countered by telling Northerners to emancipate their free blacks since there was also discrimination in the North. Alexis de Tocqueville, the French traveler and commentator, even remarked upon the greater degree of discrimination and racial prejudice in those northern states that had abolished slavery compared to those that had not.[10]

While almost all of the states north of the Mason-Dixon line did begin to institute antislavery laws or propose discussion for gradual emancipation plans, there was no commitment or implementation by any of the state governments that would lead to equality. During the first half of the nineteenth century nearly every northern state debated the issue of emancipation. Indiana, Illinois, and Oregon adopted limits on further immigration of blacks. Some states required proof of freedom for incoming blacks; in other areas, blacks had to post bond of $500 to $1,000 as evidence of future good behavior.[11] What was the free black response to this context? In 1827, a new stage of black development emerged with the founding of the first black newspaper: *Freedom's Journal*. Edited by John B. Russwurm and Samuel E. Cornish, it widened the channel of communication for blacks.[12] Local papers began to develop. The antebellum papers were not written for the slave population but for free blacks, particularly those who were relatively mobile in the northern states. The approach was self-help; the focus was upon the conditions in particular areas, black susceptibility to kidnapping, issues in the colonization controversy, and so forth.[13]

9. Berlin, *Slaves Without Masters*, chapter ten.

10. Alexis de Tocqueville, *Democracy in America*.

11. Litwack, *North of Slavery*, p. 70; Howard H. Bell, "Free Negroes of the North, 1830–1835: A Study in National Cooperation," *The Journal of Negro Education*, p. 447.

12. Bell, "Free Negroes," p. 447.

13. See Dann, *The Black Press, 1827–1890: The Quest for National Identity*, for a discussion of this point.

Of particular importance was the black convention movement that emerged in the 1830s in reaction to the deteriorating status of free blacks. The movement was influential in the black community up to the Civil War and through Reconstruction. Stemming from small-scale attempts to remove slavery and to stem the steady erosion of the few privileges granted to free blacks, the Negro Convention Movement hammered out calls for justice and reform. The first conclave in Philadelphia in 1830 was a response to repeated incidences of mob action by whites against blacks in Cincinnati. The increasing size of the black population in that city was of concern to the unskilled whites who perceived the blacks as an economic and social threat. Both legal and extralegal actions took place against blacks.[14] Initially conventions were held annually but were later called as the situation warranted. The so-called leaders of the black community, representing ad hoc organizations for the most part, were the attendants and discussants. The convention movement, appealing to solidarity and racial self-help, was a northern phenomenon for the most part since there was greater danger involved in southern black participation.[15]

But the efforts of free blacks to establish themselves as different was dysfunctional for their purposes:

> The free Negroes' fervent attempt to shake off the habits of slavery, purchase property, build churches and schools, and establish an identity as a free people heightened white fears. Ironically, the more the free Negro became like them, the more enraged whites became. It was easy for a people who professed to love freedom to despise a slave; whites needed reasons to hate blacks who were free. The growth of the free Negro caste and the development of Afro-American culture as manifested in the independent black churches and schools forced whites to define more carefully than ever the difference between free and slave, white and black. It was no accident that an articulate defense of slavery appeared with the emergence of the free Negro caste.[16]

It is in this setting that black Freemasonry was of vital impor-

14. More than half the black population in Cincinnati at that time left for Canada and other parts of the North in response to the repressive nature of the situation

15. See August Meier and Elliott Rudwick, *From Plantation to Ghetto,* pp. 104–12, for a thorough but succinct discussion of the movement. See also Bell, "Free Negroes."

16. Berlin, *Slaves Without Masters,* p. 90.

tance to the "free men of color." The heightened fear of black power provided an environmental factor for the nurturance of Freemasonry as an adaptive and protective mechanism and power source. To remain economically viable the free blacks had to neutralize their threat potential. It is suggested here that Masonic belonging, for the founding fathers of Prince Hall Freemasonry, was part of an attempt to be allowed to function uncluttered by, and emancipated from, their designated inferior status in the surrounding society.

The security aspect as an important dimension of appeal cannot be overstated.[17] Fellow Freemasons, as a status referent, offered a real and potential degree of protective coloration. The potential for a network of underlying connections between black communities, and between white and black communities via Masonic associations, was a perceived reality in the first case, an occasional occurrence in the latter. Black Masons collectively faced the onslaught of biological racism.[18]

Shades of difference between blacks and whites began to be more highly emphasized. Attempts to show biological differences of kind rather than degree proliferated. During the 1820s and through the 1840s congressional discussions defending slavery focused on the abject poverty of the unfortunate free black and the high rates of vice and even insanity or mental retardation.[19] Despite evidence that the statistics were manipulated, and that blacks were enumerated in areas having no black population, many whites remained convinced of the benign nature of slavery in the United States.

The debates from the 1840s through the 1860s concerning restrictions on the expansion of slavery westward were chiefly motivated by the desire to establish and preserve white land and labor. Antagonism over black laborers had a long history. At a 1660 Boston town meeting a discussion was held concerning barring the use of slaves for skilled crafts. In Philadelphia white

17. Note that in 1777 Massachusetts tabled a gradual emancipation plan that no doubt affected the motivation of the blacks drawn to Freemasonry. See McManus, *Black Bondage*, p. 164.

18. See William J. Wilson, *Power, Racism and Privilege*, for a useful distinction between biological and cultural racism.

19. It was in 1841 that the nadir of this reasoning appeared. The sixth census was said to have firmly established that the incidence of insanity or mental retardation among free, as contrasted with slave, blacks was eleven times higher. See Litwack, *North of Slavery*, pp. 163–68 on this point.

artisans were equally upset.[20] This antagonism from labor was a recurrent experience for blacks. In Cincinnati, the persecution of potential labor competitors, or so they were perceived, led to mob violence (whites attacking blacks) and a riot in 1829 where, for days, police were unable to restore order. More than a thousand free blacks emigrated to Canada after this attack.[21]

Initially blacks had received occupational training because of a labor shortage and the needs of an expanding economy. Wage laborers were hard to come by given the amount of land to be explored and developed. As Edgar McManus has stated: "only compulsion could maintain the stable labor force needed to provide the capital accretion for transforming the early settlements into a viable society." Thus, blacks had an economic function.[22]

In many cities of the South blacks had a relatively strong economic foundation up to this time. In Savannah, skilled artisans were hired out by their masters to rice mills, drayage firms, and construction sites. There was great occupational differentiation in the black labor force, slave and free.[23] This case example was not atypical.

The twenty years preceding the Civil War saw an intensification of worker activism stemming in part from the 1830–1860 wave of nearly five million immigrants from Europe. Newly freed skilled workers often suffered a loss in occupational status from the new competition.

Berlin categorizes a prevalent belief of this period as the positive good theory:

> If slavery was the natural state for blacks, freedom was an impossible anomaly. . . . The poverty, indolence, and criminality that whites identified with the free Negro were not the legacy of slavery or the result of white prejudice, but simply the product of the Negro's innately limited abilities. Only bondage allowed blacks to lead a normal useful life.[24]

20. See McManus, *Black Bondage,* pp. 44–45.

21. Wendell P. Dabney, *Cincinnati's Colored Citizens,* p. 35; Bell, "Free Negroes."

22. McManus, *Black Bondage,* p. 2.

23. John W. Blassingame, "Before the Ghetto: The Making of the Black Community in Savannah, Georgia, 1865–1880," *Journal of Social History,* p. 465.

24. Berlin, *Slaves Without Masters,* p. 194.

This concept of slavery as good increased concomitantly with other calls for emancipation, and still others for colonization. In response to calls for black removal from the nation, the majority of blacks pointed to the contradiction between the various schemes and professed American beliefs. Solid citizens—the white majority—disagreed for the most part.

> A Springfield, Massachusetts, Journal, discussing the question "What Shall Be Done With The Darkies?" berated Negro leaders for dereliction of duty, lack of racial pride and independence, and a tendency to cling to the coattails of white society. Colonization, it maintained, was not a degrading removal but an opportunity to build a new and constructive society.[25]

However, there were some interesting forms of black-white alliances other than that of the abolitionist movement: entrepreneurial ventures. Many "cookshops and gaming houses" were jointly owned and patronized by blacks; gangs of black and white thieves preyed upon the countryside with instances reported of whites "encouraging black criminality by establishing depots or 'night cribs' where blacks might bring stolen merchandise, find protection, or simply spend the night." Other whites saw a profit in hiding fugitive slaves.[26]

The passage by Congress of the repressive Fugitive Slave Act in 1850 reflected the degree of tension in the nation. Every free black was now legally exposed to potential capture and slave captivity. With the Dred Scott decision in 1857, the right of free blacks to claim land in the west, rarely completed, was denied.[27]

Differing estimates exist concerning the number of free blacks prior to the Civil War. By one estimate in 1860, one-seventh of the black population was free.[28] Carter Woodson estimated 488,070 to be of the "professional" class.[29] However, that figure was also quoted by the U.S. Government Printing Office in 1918 as the numerical base for the free eleven percent of the black population in 1860.[30]

25. Litwack, *North of Slavery*, p. 254; see also Bell, "Free Negroes."
26. Berlin, *Slaves Without Masters*, p. 262.
27. Bell, "Free Negroes," p. 447.
28. Harry E. Davis, *A History of Freemasonry Among Negroes in America*, p. 146.
29. Carter G. Woodson, *The Negro Professional Man*, p. 4.
30. Charles H. Wesley, *Prince Hall: Life and Legacy*, p. 30.

The New England states had only seven percent of the free blacks above the Mason-Dixon line prior to the Civil War.[31] These blacks were actively trying to overcome the increasingly restrictive development of competitive race relations with its distinctive element of blocked social, civil, and occupational mobility for the lower caste.[32]

With the beginning of the Civil War in 1861 and Lincoln's refusal to dissolve the Union, all energies by those concerned with civil rights were devoted to the possible chance of emancipation for all blacks. As contrabands became problematic, Lincoln moved from a policy of limited emancipation to full emancipation of all slaves in territory still at war with the Union. Thus, his Act of Emancipation was limited in scope, but his martyrdom two years later succeeded in making him a hero to black folk.[33]

While emancipation did free black slaves from the control of their individual masters, it left a residue of black bondage to collective mainstream society. With emancipation, black businessmen had to reevaluate their situation, as did the black skilled workers. In the former case the newly freed slaves now became customers, often not the most profitable; in the latter case white competitors no longer observed the "nigger work" barriers and started competing intensely for the same jobs. Racial tension increased significantly in the white working class.

Infragroup distinctions became more evident in the black communities. After the Civil War, one historian distinguished three major categories of persons: those who were "thrifty, intelligent and prosperous"; "secondly, those hard-working folks who had not had the advantages of the first group"; "thirdly, those who had swapped slavery for debt peonage and sharecropping."[34] While the grouping is arbitrary, it points to the diversity within the black population.

John Blassingame cites Freemasonry as one of several organi-

31. In Virginia in 1860, for example, there was one free black to every eight blacks who were slaves. In the Tidewater Region (Nansemond County), only 581 out of 2,473 blacks were slaves. See Robert Ezra Park, "Racial Assimilation in Secondary Goups," *Race and Culture.*

32. Pierre L. van den Berghe, *Race and Racism: A Comparative Perspective.*

33. See Hanes Walton, *Black Republicans: The Politics of the Black and Tans,* for a discussion of the impact of the assassination of Lincoln upon black commitment to the nineteenth-century Republican party.

34. Blassingame, "Before the Ghetto," pp. 476, 480, 485.

zations contributing to and reflecting the developing sense of unity in the first group in particular but impacting upon the entire black community as it faced the realities of emancipation:

> Nineteenth-century urban blacks had visions of the future which included self-determination, solving their social problems, educating their children and working and playing in ways which had little to do with later historians spinning fanciful theories (based on the European experience of Jews) about them being locked in "enduring ghettoes." They were building "enduring communities."[35]

This process involved the maintenance of institutional forms paralleling those of the dominant society, what is conceptualized here as pillarization. The biracial social order was functional for both personal and group support.

Historically, the black community has moved to establish and maintain formal and informal social institutions to meet the needs for services or opportunities not provided by the mainstream society. These institutions have been of invaluable strength to the diversity within the black community:

> Despite rumors to the contrary, there has been a basic unity among most blacks, which has been stronger and more fundamental than any concerns of class or caste. Despite the claim that middle class blacks have not been truly a part of this black community, there has been and continues to be a basic agreement among blacks as to fundamental goals. It is this fundamental unity which has been one great source of strength for black people.[36]

One can see this expressed in the concerns of the black Freemasons.

35. Ibid., p. 485.
36. James E. Horton, "New Directions for Research in Black History," *The Black Scholar*, p. 39. While agreeing with many of Horton's points, the author disagrees with his contention that the black experience is at odds with American history. To the contrary, it can more soundly be argued that the black experience is part and parcel of American history.

Chapter 5

The Growth of
Prince Hall Freemasonry

A major tradition within black Freemasonry has been one of activism. The founding fathers—Prince Hall, Absolum Jones, Richard Allen—and others created and developed the black body out of activism and carried their thrust for freedom throughout society. Theirs was a noble precedent for the involvement of black Masons in the betterment of society. Rather than the lodges serving as places for intellectual and abstract escape from the world, as one historian suggested,[1] they provided the setting for genuine impact on the whole black population.

It is difficult to draw the line between individual and collective Masonic activities, particularly in its first century. Masonic periodicals and documents consist mainly of moral instruction, news of meetings of subordinate lodges, obituaries, and advertisements. From time to time information can be gleaned, however, from Masonic memorabilia and documents concerning community activities. Insufficient data exists for the utilization of quantified techniques measuring proportion of the group's functioning, or finances devoted to outside interests. But by piecing together various data a pattern emerges supporting the centrality of community activism in black Masonic affairs.[2]

1. An earlier study of Prince Hall Freemasonry suggested that black Freemasonry had "throughout its history refused to participate as in institutional entity in the affairs of the community." Ample data exist to contradict this statement by William Muraskin in "Black Masons: The Role of Fraternal Orders in the Creation of a Middle-Class Black Community," Ph.D. diss., University of California-Berkeley, p. 82.

2. Of particular interest were the number of fragmentary materials, admittedly disjointed and disorganized, in the Williamson Collection on Prince Hall Freemasonry at the Schomburg Center for Research in Black Culture, The New York Public Library, New York City. Boxes of paper, both formal and informal documents, brittle with age and disuse, will soon no longer be available to researchers due to their not having been processed

Boxes of papers, formal and informal documents—often memorabilia repetitious in nature and ritualistic in content—were sifted, and information extracted, evaluated, and interpreted for this study.[3]

Black Freemasonry emerged in 1775 during a chaotic period in American history. Revolutionary fervor may have obscured its beginnings from the general community, a factor of importance for the latter charges against the organization (see chapter seven). Having internalized the Masonic duty to help others, the black Freemasons, as individuals and as a collective entity, were actively involved in the affairs of the fledgling nation. To be sure it was most pragmatic on their part to demonstrate their patriotic loyalty and goodwill, but the records from this period demonstrate the sincerity of their efforts. In 1786, when Shays's Rebellion occurred, Prince Hall offered the services of the Boston lodge as soldiers to help Governor Bowdoin maintain an orderly government. In a letter dated 16 November 1786 he stated: "We, by the Providence of God, are members of a fraternity that not only enjoins upon us to be peaceable subjects to the civil powers where we reside, but it also forbids our having concern in any plot or conspiracies against the state where we dwell."[4] Prince Hall Masons stressed their commitment to idealized American values: the virtue of honesty, unselfishness, loyalty, patriotism, and friendship. Responsibilities and duties "owed to God, our neighbor and ourselves" were of prime importance in manifesting Masonic commitment.

In 1793, a yellow fever epidemic overtook Philadelphia,

---

by modern microfilming or other standard library science techniques. Preservation of the handwritten, mimeographed, typed pamphlets, brochures, broadsheets, and personal papers of this black institution has not ranked high on the budget priorities of the New York Library. The librarians at the Schomburg, however, have admirably maintained the voluminous paraphernalia under adverse conditions.

3. Gaps exists in the available Masonic documents. Those sources available are important for extraction of information when serious restrictions on fieldwork and data exist. David C. Pitt, in *Using Historical Sources in Anthropology and Sociology,* points out that Emile Durkheim was never in Australia yet wrote insightfully on the Australian aborigines. Pitt also cites Weber's utilization of documentary records for his study of ancient India and China.

4. Harold Van Buren Voorhis, *Negro Masonry in the United States,* p. 29; Harry E. Davis, *A History of Freemasonry Among Negroes in America,* p. 431.

striking particularly hard among the white populace. A group of free blacks, headed by Absolum Jones, answered the public call for the care of the sick. It is this group that is listed in documents as the membership of the black Masonic lodge of Philadelphia.[5] Early records show that in other areas, even in the South, black Masonic lodges frequently donated their service in the relief of yellow-fever sufferers.

But black Freemasons had particular concerns, and the general value of Masonic ties had pragmatic importance. Masonic membership had real utility for blacks: it offered a measure of protection in a world where little was predictable. For example, in 1788 three free blacks, one of whom happened to be a Mason, were kidnapped off the streets of Boston after having responded to a request to aid a stricken vessel. The three were kidnapped and transported to the West Indian island of Saint Bartholomew.[6] Prince Hall, hearing of the abduction, asked for state help. He petitioned the state legislature on 27 February 1788 on behalf of black men who were continuously subject to such inhumane treatment. Hall cited the prevalence of the practice of free blacks being hired as seamen only to find themselves faced with slavery or the threat of such. A petition from the African Lodge asked for assistance in the return of the three individuals who were to be sold into slavery.[7]

As it happened, the merchant who was approached to buy the three males was himself a Freemason. The black Freemason made known by sign that he was a Mason. When the white Mason heard of the details of the capture he insisted that the ship's captain and the men be taken to see the governor of the island. The shipmaster, however, convinced the authorities that the three blacks had been purchased from a jail. Therefore, the

---

5. See Davis, *A History of Freemasonry.*

6. This manner of kidnapping was not unique. See Solomon Northrup, *Twelve Years a Slave,* for an excellent firsthand account of such a case. Northrup was a free black born in the 1840s and sold into slavery in New Orleans. His ordeal lasted twelve years. See also Linda W. Slaughter, *Freedom of the South.*

7. The signers of the petition were all members of African Lodge No. 459. See Davis, *History of Freemasonry,* p. 430. There was little in reality that could be done to prevent such kidnappings. Legally, the hands of blacks were tied for, with the exception of Delaware, no blacks were allowed to testify in court against whites. Thus, the victim, if released, had no defense.

black men were detained further until proof to the contrary could be obtained. When the proof did arrive, as did supportive Masonic letters, the men were liberated.[8]

Black Masons frequently state that Masonic membership through the decades and centuries has been of survival importance in times of stress. Examples are cited of the cessation of mob beatings and lynchings when one of the leaders caught the Masonic signal of distress. But pragmatic survival concerns are only one aspect of the story.

From the start of black Freemasonry, members were involved in community uplift. As Saunders Redding noted: "The Boston lodge was wide awake on matters of general welfare."[9] The education of black children was a particular social concern of these black Masons. In 1786 Prince Hall, Lancaster Hill, Nero Brewster, and other Masons petitioned the Massachusetts legislature for educational facilities for black children.[10] The petition was denied, but in 1789, due to Masonic efforts, the first black public school in the United States was opened at No. 8 Smith Court in Boston. It had taken years of petitioning, followed by the solicitation of funds from prominent and powerful individuals. Prince Saunders, secretary of African Lodge No. 459, one of the first black college graduates, became the teacher at the school.[11]

The pattern was set for future generations of black Masons. The major principles of Freemasonry call for belief and behavior in accordance with the "Great Architect of the Universe"[12] and nonparticipation in political controversy. The manner by which political controversy has been defined by black Masonic leaders

8. The Prince Hall archives contain such letters as the one written by the white Masons of Portland, Maine, No. 1 Lodge, requesting that the captured black men be freed and returned. See Davis, *History of Freemasonry*, p. 430; see also Voorhis, *Negro Masonry in the United States*, p. 28.

9. Saunders Redding, *They Came in Chains*, p. 139.

10. See Voorhis, *Negro Masonry in the United States*, p. 27.

11. See Davis, *History of Freemasonry*, p. 431. It is particularly fitting that in 1973 a new Philadelphia elementary school was named after Prince Hall. See Randall Butts, "A New School Named 'Prince Hall.'"

12. One critic of Freemasonry, a former member, takes umbrage with this concept, saying it is derogatory to God's creative omnipotence, for an architect uses only materials already at hand. He designs, but he does not create. See Walton Hannah, *Darkness Visible: A Revelation and Interpretation of Freemasonry*, p. 34.

leaves ample room for commitment to social causes. Nothing in the Landmarks of Masonry, it has been interpreted, restricts Masons to being passive citizens: "There are plenty of references in both ritual and monitor to our being good citizens and loyal citizens. But the best citizens are not always the passive ones . . . the great Christian Exemplar himself grew militant when occasion demanded."[13] Further support for the legitimacy of Masonic activism is that the Mason is instructed to labor for the benefit of mankind and to view charity as the chief virtue. Thus, the thin line between nonpolitical involvement and loyalty to more activism for civil rights over the years has been an easy one for black Masons to resolve. Their commitment to social justice falls well within the boundaries of exemplification of Masonic enlightenment.

An 1802 report by African Lodge No. 459 listed eight Masons as having died and eighteen as entering since 1797. Between 1808 and 1824 there were, in addition, eighty candidates. The minutes for the years between 1807 and 1846 show more than 450 meetings.[14] Black Freemasonry was swiftly spreading.

Prince Hall, functioning as provincial grand master, granted a warrant in 1797 to a Philadelphia body consisting of several members who were already Ancient York Masons, having been initiated in London or Ireland.[15] Among these as master was Absolum Jones, the first black priest of the Episcopal church; as treasurer, Richard Allen, the founder and first bishop of the African Methodist Episcopal Church.

In 1797 another lodge was constituted centering around members of the Boston lodge residing in Rhode Island. Hiram Lodge No. 3 of Providence existed for only two decades before the body became dormant in 1813, when most of the members migrated to Liberia via the African Humane Society.[16]

Prince Hall Freemasonry, so designated after the death of the first black Masonic leader, spread rapidly as the accompanying

13. See Ray V. Denslow, *Regular, Irregular, and Clandestine Grand Lodges: A Study in Foreign Recognition,* p. 43.
14. Voorhis, *Negro Masonry in the United States,* p. 30.
15. Ibid., p. 32; Davis, *History of Freemasonry,* p. 95, contends that there were black Masons in Philadelphia possibly before Prince Hall received his warrant, but that these Masons were unable to receive dispensation from local Masons and thus turned to the northern black body.
16. Voorhis, *Negro Masonry in the United States,* p. 34.

chart suggests. However, one should not assume that it was easy for free blacks to join together in any organizational form. Assembly was restricted in some areas.[17]

The question arises as to whether white Freemasons supported the growth and spread of Prince Hall Freemasonry, and whether they assisted in smoothing the ways for black groups to function within local communities. White Masons sometimes warned Prince Hall Masons, forbidden by law to congregate, of impending raids. In Alexandria, Virginia, before emancipation, they were not only warned, but if by any chance black Masons were found congregating, then white Masonic judges would free them.[18]

Another incident is told of the value of Masonic affiliation in contravening the controls of segregation. Mt. Morah Lodge No. 1 of Louisville, Kentucky, had been warranted in 1850, but the black codes did not allow assembly in that city. The group, therefore, met in New Albany, Indiana, for three years. The lodge decided to take a stand and meet in Louisville, but the lodge rooms were raided and twenty-one black persons arrested. But the jailer was a white Mason and released the men on their own recognizance. On the following day when the men appeared at the courthouse they found several policemen waiting for them with pleasant news: they were told to depart quietly and not speak of the incident.[19] Further, some documentation exists that white Masons visited black lodges from time to time. In 1799 and 1800, the Philadelphia black Masonic records document ten white Masons as visitors.[20] Placing these instances in balance, however, one notes that blacks extended their fellowship and visitation rites to whites but rarely was the reverse true, and only on a limited and exceptional personage basis.[21]

---

17. See Winthrop Jordan, *White Over Black: American Attitudes Toward the Negro, 1550–1812,* p. 398. For a more thorough discussion of the problem of free blacks, see also John Hope Franklin, *From Slavery to Freedom: A History of American Negroes.*

18. See Davis, *History of Freemasonry,* p. 2.

19. Ibid., pp. 151–52.

20. Ibid., p. 97. See also Harry A. Williamson, *A History of Freemasonry Among the American Negroes,* for examples of individual white Masons taking action on behalf of black Masonry.

21. One known exception to this was a subordinate lodge in Brooklyn that admitted black visitors occasionally and returned their visits.

Blacks have known well that the universal brotherhood of Masonic affiliation was often an abstraction removed from the daily life of black and white Masons.

While Georg Simmel suggests that secret societies "offer a very impressive schooling in the moral solidarity among men,"[22] the morality may not be universally internalized or acted upon. Despite the ideology of Freemasonry, separate lodges have existed for centuries and continue to exist.

By the time of emancipation, the Prince Hall affiliates had lodges in fourteen states, most of these on the Atlantic coast as far south as the District of Columbia, in southern Louisiana, the Midwest, and Canada.[23] Prince Hall Freemasonry as a separate but parallel body also spread to the islands of the Caribbean. Black lodges, for example, have been a part of black communities in Bermuda since 1838.[24]

The period of the convention movement saw a spectacular increase in black Masonic lodges as black institutions in general grew in strength and determination. Employment and wages were high despite the obstacles stemming from the various laws imposed by the authorities. Land values increased, affecting those free middle-class landowners. Most importantly, black consciousness of the growing sectional dispute in the 1850s, and the awareness of the potential in any change, generated a new sense of group pride. In turn, white fear of black retaliation again reached new heights.

As can be seen by the accompanying chart, there was a phenomenal emergence of Prince Hall lodges in the three years following the cessation of the Civil War. This was the period of

22. Georg Simmel, "The Secret and The Secret Society," in *The Sociology of Georg Simmel,* pp. 307–76.

23. It is not striking that Louisiana had lodges prior to the Civil War. The different regional variation in interpretation of free black status no doubt explains this phenomenon since this part of the country was settled by French and Spanish settlers. "As a general rule, Lower South free Negroes were not only more urban and light skinned, but better educated, more skilled, and more closely connected with whites, than those of the Upper South," writes Berlin, *Slaves Without Masters,* p. 181. Compare Jordan, *White Over Black,* chapter two.

24. Odd Fellows, Shepherds, and Samaritans were also early fraternal fellowships in Bermuda. When the first black church, belonging to the African Methodist Episcopal denomination, was formed in 1870, the services were held in a Masonic lodge hall. See Frank E. Manning, *Black Clubs in Bermuda: Ethnography of a Play World.*

Founding of First Prince Hall Lodges by State

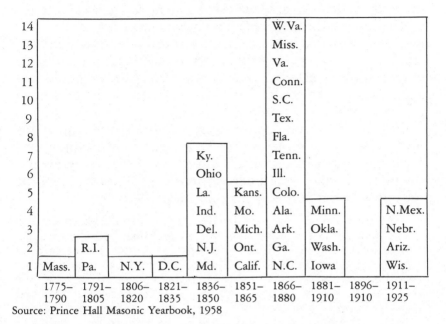

Source: Prince Hall Masonic Yearbook, 1958

hope for blacks that led to the first, and only, period of black political power. The Grand Lodge of Illinois, organized in 1867, had fifteen Prince Hall subordinate lodges in Chicago alone in 1885, with many community leaders as members.[25] The Reconstruction years were good ones for black Freemasonry.

Hope was revived that white Masonry would remove the restrictive practices against black persons. The Civil War had accentuated the confusion over the status of black Masons despite the hope generated among the Prince Hall lodges that with emancipation would come a more liberal attitude. But, "on the contrary, in some Masonic jurisdictions legislation of a prohibitive nature was passed upon the admitting of Negroes to the Fraternity. . . . The general attitude of the Craft, as a whole, however, was to look upon Freemasonry as a province of white men."[26] The legitimacy of black Freemasonry was still not recognized.

After the Civil War there was some discussion among a more liberal minority of white Masons in widely separated areas about

25. The Odd Fellows had six at that time. See Allan Spear, *Black Chicago: The Making of a Negro Ghetto, 1890–1920.*
26. Voorhis, *Negro Masonry in the United States,* p. 77.

adherence to the ideals espoused on universal brotherhood. In New Jersey, for example, where the grand lodge accepted several blacks into the mainstream body with much fanfare from the media, controversies extended over several years over the fact that black members had been accepted by regular subordinate lodges. Some local lodges protested vigorously any other lodge's admittance or initiation of blacks as "disturbing the peace and harmony of the institution."[27]

Other state grand lodges decried further opening of the brotherhood, and some, such as Delaware and Mississippi, severed Masonic relations (official interchange) with the New Jersey Grand Lodge. In a letter written in 1908 terminating the relationship, the Mississippi grand master wrote:

> Masonry never contemplated that her privileges should be extended to a race, totally, morally and intellectually incapacitated to discharge the obligations which they assume or have conferred upon them in a Masonic lodge. It is no answer that there are exceptions to this general character of the race. We legislate for the race and not for the exceptions. We hold that affiliation with negroes is contrary to the teachings of Masonry, and is dangerous to the interest of the Fraternity of Free and Accepted Masons.[28]

Ambivalence was also present among individual Masons. In one ironic incident, the superintendent of the Freedmen's Bureau equivocated: "as an officer of the United States" he had no prejudices at all against blacks, "but as a Mason and a member of a North Carolina Chapter, I do most decidedly object to their being made Masons, provided they are not 'free born.' "[29] Schizophrenic equivocation over black Freemasonry has had a long history in America, as has the racial paradox of parallel structures.

27. Ibid., p. 84.
28. Ibid., p. 101. It was not until 1928, twenty years later, that Masonic relations between theses two states were reinstituted.
29. See the letter written in 1866, quoted in Voorhis, *Negro Masonry in the United States*, p. 120.

Chapter 6

The Masonic Realities

The history of mainstream Freemasonry's relationship with various minority groups reflects societal patterns of discrimination against those groups whose relative powerlessness rests upon an ascribed and devalued characteristic. One observer has noted that the "history of Masonic emancipation is a mirror clearly reflecting the problems inherent in civil emancipation."[1] Masonic lodges, ironically referred to by members as "morality institutions,"[2] have reflected the mores and values of the larger society. The egalitarianism of Masonic precepts is challenged by the experience of interaction between the white body and black Freemasonry, the Mormon, Native American, and Chinese experiences, and the Jewish experience with European Freemasonry.

Before reviewing these experiences, however, we must fully understand the nature of Masonic philosophy and practice. Freemasonry as a long-standing institution is not of sociological significance for its outer appearance, whether exotic or stolid. Too often the historic importance of Freemasonry as a world influence has been neglected. As J. M. Roberts notes: "[It] is one of the most important, as well as one of the most underrated of English cultural influences on Europe in the last two-and-a-half centuries. The structure of lodges, their subordination to grand lodges, the three grades, ideological latitudinarianism and the social prestige of freemasonry were all to spread over the world."[3] Within every social world there is a special universe of discourse, a particular manner of categorizing experiences, a unique set of symbols and referents, and a general worldview.

1. Jacob Katz, *Jews and Freemasons in Europe, 1723–1939*, p. 4. See also Frank Hankins, "Masonry," *Encyclopedia of the Social Sciences*, vol. ten, p. 183.
2. Noel Gist, "Secret Societies: Cultural Study of Fraternalism in the United States," *The University of Missouri Studies*, p. 142.
3. J. M. Roberts, *The Mythology of the Secret Societies*, p. 30.

The meaning of Masonic doctrine and ritual, it is astutely held by members, is not revealed by one-dimensional words; the subjective experience the members share provides the substance and import of membership. Emile Durkheim discussed the importance of symbols for social unity thusly: ". . . the emblem is not merely a convenient process for clarifying the sentiment society has of itself: it also served to create this sentiment; it is one of its constituent elements." The ritualized use of the emblems inform the members "that they are in harmony," thus making them "conscious of their moral unity. It is by uttering the same cry, pronouncing the same word, or performing the same gesture in reward to some object that they become and feel themselves in unison."[4] Masons zealously attempt to preserve the secrets of what is termed "the craft." The terminology refers back to medieval times and to the highly skilled masonry of that day. The lodge, the place where Masons meet, refers to the building where workmen ate and rested while spending years and decades on particular cathedrals or castles. The lodge was the repository for tools and implements and the place for supportive shelter. Medieval masonry workers spent seven years in apprenticeship training. It must be remembered that there were no architects as we know them, so the mason was a professionally trained and esteemed worker. The work method was kept secret, concealed to keep the practices of the craft among those suitably trained.[5]

There is no evidence that Freemasons have been working masons in the literal sense since the seventeenth century. However, the prestige of working masons who built the magnificent stone edifices of Europe, and the hope for transmitted luster and wisdom, is a tradition stemming from the guild. The Masonic

4. Emile Durkheim, *The Elementary Forms of the Religious Life,* p. 262. See also Otto's use of the term *numinous* to designate that which eludes comprehension and transcends verbal expression, in Rudolf Otto, *The Idea of the Holy.*

5. At the time when cathedrals and religious buildings took decades to build, the first step in the project consisted in the erection of a hall or lodge at the construction site where the workmen could take shelter in bad weather, store their tools, eat their meals, and, in some cases, live during the progress of the construction. Henry L. Stillson and William J. Hughan, eds., *History of the Ancient and Honorable Fraternity of Free and Accepted Masons and Concordant Orders,* p. xix.

way of life and conception of the world involves learning the degree requirements, material suitable for each stage of the progression up the hierarchy of Masonic education and role performance. It is not instruction in the usual sense of objective, logical categories of new information: the degree requirements involve paradigmatic instruction geared to engender a spiritual awakening and moral functioning.

Freemasonry provides a comprehensive role system. There are various official positions and numerous opportunities for appointment to various lodge committees. Typically one finds the following at the grand lodge level: grand master, grand secretary, grand treasurer, deputy grand master, grand senior warden, grand junior warden, grand trustees, district deputy grand masters, grand lecturers, grand orator, grand chaplains, grand marshall, grand historian, grand senior deacon, grand junior deacon, grand standard bearer, grand sword bearer, and grand titler. All previous holders of the position add "past" to their title. Each subordinate lodge has a comparable hierarchy providing channels for the upwardly mobile Mason.

The elaborate setting of the lodge room and the costuming involved in lodge ceremonies heighten the significance of upward movement through the ranks. The elaborate setting legitimizes the ritual acts conducted and reinforces the import of adherence to Masonic ideals.[6] The actions are made appropriate to and by the setting. Other elements also heighten the shared experience for Masonic members. The very structure of the language and the phrasing add to the mystique, as in the case of religious procedures.[7] *Brother* is utilized as it has been by religious groups, guilds, and trades for centuries. In Freemasonry, as in earlier and present usage, *brother* implies kinship and kinship obligations created by the sharing of difficult experiences.

The ritualized initiation cements the solemmity of member-

6. Noise and lighting are also used for creating an impression and for impact.

7. Examining Freemasonry as a religious institution obscures the true nature of the organization and, further, misses the point of its social importance. Religion and secrecy do share certain commonalities, however: both are concerned with the nonempirical and the nonscientific; both have symbolic and sacred components; both are ritualized; both have hierarchical elements.

ship in a society having secrets known only to the selected. During the first-degree ceremony, the initiate is taught the importance of secrecy:

> Secrecy consists in an inviolable adherence to the obligation you have entered into, never improperly to disclose any of those Masonic secrets which have now been, or may, at any future period, be entrusted to your keeping, and cautiously to avoid all occasions which may inadvertently lead you to do so. Your fidelity must be exemplified by a strict observance of the Constitution of the Fraternity, by adhering to the ancient landmarks of the Order, by never attempting to extort or otherwise unduly obtain the secrets of a superior degree and by refraining from recommending anyone to a participation of our secrets unless you have strong grounds to believe that by a similar fidelity he will ultimately reflect honor on your choice. Your obedience must be proved by a strict observance of our laws and regulations, by prompt attention to all signs and summonses, by modest and correct demeanor in the lodge . . .[8]

The ritual pledge, an expressive mechanism fostering integration, heightens the sense of being among a select group of influentials. Perhaps it is the "passion of secrecy," as Simmel suggests,[9] that irrespective of particular content, helps to give the group form and significance. The initiation rite is the symbolic deepening of an important transformation that leads to the acceptance of a new, affirmed image of self. Mircea Eliade has pointed out that all premodern societies have placed great importance on the ideology and techniques of status change via the process of initiation.[10] There is also a strong play element involved. While the essential feature of ritual is that something out of the ordinary "calculated to arouse admiration," it is also a stepping away from common reality into a different and higher level.[11] The symbols of Freemasonry also represent status

8. Quoted in James Dewar, *The Unlocked Secret: Freemasonry Examined,* p. 96.

9. Georg Simmel, "The Secret and the Secret Society," in *The Sociology of Georg Simmel,* ed. and trans., Kurt H. Wolff, p. 363.

10. Mircea Eliade, in *Rites and Symbols of Initiation,* discussed two major types of initiations: collective rituals occurring to everyone passing a certain age and *mannerbund,* mystical vocation rituals such as those of secret societies. Freemasonry involves the second type, a progressive transformation of a community of initiates.

11. Johan Huizinga, *Homo Ludens,* p. 33. The importance of the play element in secret ritual has ancient roots. For example, Huizinga discusses how in the ancient Chinese tradition music and dance are thought to

change and progression. The symbolism of the stone is an example. A rough stone is symbolic of man in infancy. A polished stone, literally and figuratively, is a sign of a virtuous man of achievement.[12]

There are strict requirements for acceptance as a Mason, stricter than the mere ability to hold to an oath of secrecy. The individual must be nominated or recommended by a member and must have achieved some measure of economic success and community visibility or popularity viewed as evidence of good moral character. The character of the nominee is investigated by a three-man group appointed by the subordinate lodge to serve for one year. The candidate must be assessed as a man of honor, intelligent and free from any bodily defect that would prevent him from carrying out his Masonic duties. The investigatory committee reports its findings to the general body, which then must decide to accept or reject the potential novice. Each member of a lodge has a vote, and one vote against means the applicant is rejected.[13] The potential for unfair discriminatory rejection exists.

There are various systems within Freemasonry. The Scottish Rite rituals are a cumulative body of philosophically based procedures. The popularity of these rituals is said to stem from: the prestige of the innovators, French immigrants and travelers to America; the small number of persons required for the conduction of these rites; the swiftness with which one can move up the Masonic ladder.[14] Another system, that of Sym-

---

function to keep the balance between the world and nature at an optimal level of benefit for humankind.

12. Compare Thomas Luckmann, *The Invisible Religion,* pp. 44–45: "Meaning is not an inherent quality of subjective processes but is bestowed on it in interpretive acts . . . The meaningful quality of subjective experience . . . is a product of social processes." See also Harvey Cox, *The Seduction of the Spirits: The Use and Misuse of People's Religion.*

13. There are no hereditary rights in Freemasonry. Membership cannot overtly be passed from father to son. In reality, men of honor look with favor upon the sons of men of honor.

14. Different theories exist as to the origins of the Scottish Rites. Substantial evidence suggests that Chevalier Michall Ramsey, a loyal partisan of the Stuarts when France was in the "throes of a craze for things esoteric and occult," both an honest man and a charlatan, assembled and recombined earlier ritual work. Constitutions in mainstream Masonry in 1762 and 1786 legitimated the tradition. See Harry E. Davis, "The Scottish Rite in the Prince Hall Fraternity."

bolic Degrees, is also considered prestigious. Both systems, which involve fee assessments for degree advancement, are found within white and black Freemasonry, as is the elite sub-grouping within the institution: the Shriners.

To be a Shriner is an indication of Masonic eliteness and evidence of a pattern of achievement within the brotherhood. Membership in this group, renowned for charity and conviviality, is the highest status.[15] A young doctor in New York, Walter Millard Fleming, wrote the ritual for what was to become the Ancient Arabic Order, Nobles of the Mystic Shrine for North America, now more than 800,000 strong (mainstream). The Shriners cater to the more monied Masonic members; initiation and annual fees are costly. The prestige and status gains apparently offer adequate compensation to the members. Thirteen black men in Chicago established the black Shriners in 1893. Other temples emerged in Los Angeles, Washington, D. C., Jacksonville, Kansas City, and a few other cities.

Irrespective of degree and systems, Masons stress responsibility to one another and to the community. As one communiqué stated: "We should all strive to strengthen our ties with one another, visit the sick, assist the afflicted and contribute our share toward the help and care of widows and orphans."[16] The idealized American values of honesty, unselfishness, and loyalty to family and country, are said to be the bases for action.

Each grand lodge is autonomous. This, some maintain, dilutes the potential impact of the body. Simmel held that the Freemasonry of his time was of lesser impact on society that it could potentially have been due to the loose structure of Masonry: "Freemasonry, probably, owes the evident lag in its power behind its diffusion and means, to the considerable autonomy of its parts, which have neither a unified organization nor a central authority."[17] Others disagree, arguing that the impact of Freemasonry stems from individual manifestation of

15. One respondent described it as "the good time part of Masonry." Fred Van Deventer's *Parade to Glory* presents a description of mainstream Shriners. The author speaks of the organization as the playground and showcase of Masonry. No mention is made in the book of black Shriners.

16. Robert C. Garnett, Jr., compiler, *Proceedings of the Most Worshipful Prince Hall Grand Lodge*, p. 27.

17. Simmel, "The Secret and the Secret Society," p. 371.

the canons of Freemasonry. The Masonic lodge exercises control of its members by several means: approval of initial membership, taxation, threat of expulsion, fines, and reprimands. The possibility of embarrassment is a concomitant of membership in the lodge. Grievance procedures do exist: the member has a right to trial by a court of fraternal peers in particular instances. At the other extreme, honorary degrees and awards are group mechanisms to reward the true practitioner.[18]

But what has been the community perception of the practices of Freemasonry? Has Masonry always been perceived as a positive organization? It certainly has not always been viewed with public favor. The first colonial attack on Freemasonry appeared in the *New York Gazette* in 1737.[19] The article assailed the secret nature of the meetings and accused the members of immoral practices. Oaths, particularly those using the threat of death for disclosure of Masonic secrets, were suspect. Secrecy was equated with something negative to hide; if not immoral, at least conspiratorial.

A Philadelphia paper also began to write of Masons as persons engaging in lewd and immoral practices. The impetus for the attack seems to have been an accident that occurred during an initiation ceremony at a local lodge. A novice was burned during the incident and subsequently died. Three members of the lodge were tried and convicted of manslaughter. After their conviction, Benjamin Franklin's paper reported that the three men were not real members but had only posed as such. Franklin, an active Mason, evidently felt it his duty to defend Freemasonry by countering the attacks by the rival paper.[20]

Anti-Masonic sentiment was politically manipulatable, providing a scapegoat in times of social change. Wilson Carey McWilliams claimed that anti-Masonry was a diversion from the more logical villain: the commercial order.[21] The secrecy and exclusivity of Masonry was viewed by some as tinged with

18. The following section is based largely on the comprehensive and definitive study by Lorman Ratner, *Antimasonry: The Crusade and the Party*.
19. This was the first article written in the colonies. Some papers had previously reprinted articles appearing in England detailing distrust of Freemasonry.
20. See Melvin M. Johnson, *The Beginnings of Freemasonry in America*.
21. Wilson Carey McWilliams, *The Idea of Fraternity in America*.

heresy and was thus suspicious in the eyes of the traditionalism of the eighteenth century.

In 1790, anti-Masonic feeling ran high. Some antagonists held that Masons fomented religious and political revolt. This, it must be recalled, was a time when war with France seemed inevitable. It was also a period when little respect was being shown to the new country. Internally there were power struggles over foreign policy. Political clubs were forming to challenge the power of the Federalists. Francis Granger, Thurlow Weed, Millard Fillmore, and John Quincy Adams (an ex-Mason) became members of the Anti-Masonic party, holding their first general convention in Leroy, New York, in 1882.[22] The Catholic church also heavily denounced Freemasonry as a "tool of atheists and revolutionaries," challenging both church and state in their pursuits of reform by reason.

Precipitating the largest outpouring of anti-Masonic sentiment was the kidnapping of William Morgan from the Batavia, New York, jail in 1826. It was said that three men took him by force from the jail. One man named Lawson and two others were eventually tried for abduction but acquitted. Morgan's body was never recovered. Who was this man and why was his disappearance a matter of national concern?

A mason by trade, Morgan was poorly educated but very articulate. Although he could not prove he had been previously initiated into Freemasonry, he was persuasive enough to be admitted into the Leroy lodge. He and others petitioned to start a lodge in a neighboring town, Batavia, but were turned down.

Morgan, a heavy drinker, was suspected of planning an unauthorized publication of the secret rituals in collaboration with David Miller, the editor of the Republican weekly, *Advocate,* in Batavia. Efforts were made to stop the publication, and Morgan, being financially embarrassed, did turn over part of the manuscript. This was not sufficient. There was talk around town of breaking into Miller's office to retrieve the remainder of the manuscript. A fire damaged the newspaper office. Simultaneously, Morgan was arrested for allegedly failing to return clothing and money that he had borrowed. The mystery begins here,

22. See Ratner, *Antimasonry,* for a fuller discussion of this point. See also Henry L. Stillson and William J. Hughan, eds., *History of the Ancient and Honorable Fraternity;* William L. Stone, *Letters on Masonry and Anti-Masonry Addressed to the Honorable John Quincy Adams.*

for it is said that when Morgan's wife went to the jail to arrange for her husband's release by turning over the entire manuscript, she was told that the debt had been paid and that Morgan had been released. He never returned home.

These events occurred at a time of expansion in the western New York area, a time when the citizens saw the leaders of the community as monopolizing all possible advantages. The issue of publication of Masonic secrets, although it would not be the first, became a cause célèbre. The circumstances of Morgan's strange disappearance were used as an indication of the privilege and stranglehold held by the powerful leaders, who were Masons.[23] Reactions ranged from approval to kill the kidnappers to denunciation of all Masons, from investigations by state legislatures to the formation of political groups.

Anti-Jacksonian and anti-Jeffersonian politicians tapped the antagonistic feelings toward Masonry and shaped a wider mass appeal in support of their doctrines. McWilliams cites the transformation of John Quincy Adams from an active Mason into a duly elected anti-Mason in 1831. The same transformation occurred with Thaddeus Stevens.[24]

Cries went out against corruption in high places and against the alleged Masonic hold on legislative and judicial processes. Organizations from the village level upward began to mobilize against the immoral Masonic movement. Evangelistic churches took up the cause. Fifteen avowed anti-Masons were elected to state political office in New York in the year 1828.[25]

Isolationism rather than inclusive Christianity is evidenced in the clerical opposition to the Masons. Parishioners were admonished to abstain from association with sinners and those of

23. It is of interest that the Morgan disappearance and accompanying uproar occurred near the time and place of Joseph Smith's founding of the Mormon church. For a fuller discussion, see Ratner, *Antimasonry*. Discussion of the Morgan event can be found in Stillson and Hughan, *History of the Ancient and Honorable Fraternity*, part 1, division 11; Stone, *Letters on Masonry*; Fred L. Pick and G. Norman Knight, *The Pocket History of Freemasonry*. Another intriguing piece of history: Morgan's widow became a Mormon and lived in Nauvoo where she later married a prominent Mormon leader and Mason. Lucinda Pendleton Morgan Harris later became "sealed" (plurally married) to Joseph Smith. See Jerald Tanner and Sandra Tanner, *Mormonism: Shadow or Reality,* chapter eleven.

24. McWilliams, *The Idea of Fraternity in America,* pp. 154–56.

25. Whitney T. Cross, *The Burned-Over District: The Social and Intellectual History of Enthusiastic Religion in Western New York 1800–1850,* p. 116.

lower sorts who congregrated in secret societies.[26] These persons were nefarious agitators, it was said. One minister preached that the Civil War "was concocted by slave holding Freemasons and their sympathizers, North as well as South."[27]

The degree to which these opinions were shared cannot be directly assessed. However, the fact that sermons such as these were printed and circulated suggests their strength among a literate segment of the population. Masons were portrayed as putting their loyalty to their fellow members ahead of loyalty to the state, allowing corruption to seep into particular matters, as with the Morgan case, and in general matters, as in state affairs. Freemasonry was also challenged for its impropriety in serving as a churchlike institution to its members. As one historian noted: "Its titles and rituals smacked of monarchy as well as of infidelity. The very secrecy which required such reckless guarding suggested ignoble and dangerous designs."[28] Detailed descriptions of alleged immorality can be found in the anti-Masonic literature. David Brian Davis placed this literature as part of a general nativistic literature consisting of three different trends: anti-Masonic, anti-Catholic, and anti-Mormon. All three, he argued can best be interpreted as "a projection of forbidden desires" because of the exaggeration of the stereotyped enemy's power. Masonic, Catholic, and Mormon leaders were all portrayed as never hindered by conscience or respect for traditional morality. Davis found that they were also portrayed as "curiously superior to ordinary Americans in cunning, in exercising power over others, and especially in captivating gullible women."[29] These characteristics were imputed to members of all three groups, yet there was never any mention of black Freemasonry.

Anti-Masonry, a white phenomenon, was complicated, for

26. Two examples: Joel Wakeman, "A Sermon on the Nature and Tendencies of Secret Societies," delivered at Prattsburg, New York, on 25 January 1847; Rev. M. S. Drury, "Secrecy and Its Relation to the Family, State and Church," Address before the Iowa Anti-Secrecy Association, 26 April 1876.

27. Drury, "Secrecy," p. 1.

28. Cross, *The Burned-Over District,* p. 119.

29. David Brian Davis, "Some Themes of Counter-Subversion: An Analysis of Anti-Masonic, Anti-Catholic, and Anti-Mormon Literature," *Mississippi Valley Historical Review,* p. 217.

here the offensive group, known to be old stock with well-established ties in American society, was being defined as un-American. The paradox was not to last long, undoubtedly due to the positions of leverage held by individual Masons. While both anti-Catholicism and anti-Mormonism extended into the twentieth century, anti-Masonry flared more rapidly but was demolished more readily than the other two.

Similarities in perceptions of a threat can be extracted from the nineteenth-century literature. All three came to visibility in the Northeast around the same time. Anti-Mormonism did not result in a political party as did the other two, primarily because of the greater commitment of Mormons to their own belief system and daily affairs.[30] However, Freemasonry was viewed as only marginally more secretive than Jesuitism, and Brigham Young was portrayed as equal to the pope in terms of influence upon behavior. Cabalistic beliefs were strong, holding that the leaders of Catholicism, Mormonism, and Freemasonry were in collusion despite outward appearances, brutally indoctrinating their members in immorality in an attempt to gain control of the United States and the world. The leaders were characterized in terms of the un-American traits of secrecy and selfishness; members were portrayed as blindly obedient to their organizations.

Davis interprets this nineteenth-century fear as "essentially an inverted image of Jacksonian democracy and the cult of the common man."[31] With social democracy apparently attainable, uneasiness began to surface: how was an individual to gauge the trustworthiness of those with whom he or she must deal? While wanting to believe in the freedoms of the Jacksonian era, nativists worried that these would turn into license for those not as loyal as themselves. The argument was commonly stated in terms of America being a completely and perfectly free country, obviating the necessity for the existence of any organized secrecy. Popular sovereignty assured all the freedoms one could desire. Why, then, should anyone choose to keep secret his activities unless they were injurious to the harmony of all?

30. For this, the fledgling Republican party officially castigated Mormonism in 1856. See Davis, "Some Themes of Counter-Subversion," p. 206.

31. Ibid., p. 208.

Legitimate spheres of privacy were difficult to define or accept when there was uncertainty over the realm of public interest and one's place in the developing society.[32]

Complicating public fears of Freemasonry was the group's usage of figurative language and symbolism intertwined with secrecy. Room for misunderstanding existed since the entire morality system of Freemasonry was veiled in allegory. Masons attempted to dispel public fear by arguing that the order has no secret aims but is, instead, a private organization with good intentions:

> Freemasonry is not, strictly speaking, a secret society, for it has neither secret aims nor constituents. Everywhere its laws may be perused by "friend and foe" alike, and its objects are exclusively those which are, and always have been, published to the world. It is private rather than secret; for unless it be our esoteric customs, which relate, directly or indirectly, to our universal and special modes of recognition, we have no secrets.[33]

Masons repeatedly maintained that the oaths they took did not interfere with religious or political principles common to the larger society.

It has been suggested that the anti-Masonic movement may have been the first organized expression of "rural jealousy of urban superiority, or at least toward the controlling middle class of the larger villages and country towns."[34] The movement spoke to this but also to the many different anxieties of the time, a period of social change. In western New York, the rural and lower class utilized the issue to create a more positive image of their moral superiority compared to the economically better-off middle class. Even the clergy felt called upon to take overt steps beyond sermonizing against the Masons: more laymen were

32. Ibid., p. 211.
33. Stillson and Hughan, *History of the Ancient and Honorable Fraternity*, p. xvi.
34. Cross, *The Burned-Over District*, p. 117. During a period of six years, 140 anti-Masonic newspapers were founded. See Dewar, *The Unlocked Secret*. Rochester, New York, for example, was an early center of such journalism. Cross argues that the particular context of agricultural trade and fecundity, combined with the moral intensity of the "burnt-over district," provided the necessary ingredient to "elevate" and escalate the moral indignation. Many lodges closed as businessmen found their Masonic membership detrimental to their profit margin.

allowed into decisionmaking positions with the church, an unintended benefit.

The Anti-Masonic party, noteworthy because it was the first third party in the United States, and the first political party to set forth an explicit program, ended with the election of 1832.[35] That the election could signal the end of formal or major protest suggests that the major objection to Freemasonry was not the secrecy but the exclusivity. If secrecy had been the prime offender, there would not have been the superabundance of additional prestigious secret societies. As Arthur Schlesinger has commented, it is in keeping with the spirit of democracy that more secret societies were formed so that there would be enough for all to join.[36]

Perceptions of the brotherhood as a threat lessened after this. The members, once discriminated against themselves, could begin to look to the internal paradoxes in their midst, such as the denial of recognition of Prince Hall Freemasonry.[37] Prince Hall Freemasonry had escaped the anti-Masonic sentiment from outsiders. As a whole, white Masons failed to understand that they too were discriminators.

35. Carl N. Degler, *Out of Our Past: The Forces That Shaped Modern America*, p. 142.

36. Arthur Schlesinger, "Biography of a Nation of Joiners," *American Historical Review*, p. 12.

37. Recognition, in the Masonic framework, refers to a specific procedure ideologically and institutionally based. Its official meaning is an indication of "solemn and formal kinship." Harry E. Davis., *A History of Freemasonry Among Negroes in America*, p. 110.

Chapter 7

The Discrepancy in
Universalism: Minorities

It has been noted by a Prince Hall spokesman that "in Masonic, as well as in political history, the Negro has been the vortex around which a veritable torrent of passion has whirled."[1] The vortex can be extended further to other minority groups: Jews, Indians, Chinese, Mormons, and immigrants for a time were excluded or treated as inferior by white Freemasons. Little data exists on the experience of American Jews with Freemasonry in the United States, but the European experience has been studied in detail.[2] For purposes of enlightenment, a short review of minority experiences will be briefly presented.

The first Jewish Masons were said to be "educated individuals endeavoring to lighten the oppressiveness of their Judaism and to mitigate the feeling of isolation that had overtaken them."[3] As was the case with the early hopeful yearnings of the original black Freemasons in America, some Jews were attracted to the idealism of Freemasonry. They, too, were excluded from the supposedly universal brotherhood.

The first recorded date of the admittance of a Jew to a Masonic lodge was 1732.[4] Some measure of early tolerance within white European Freemasonry can be assumed by the appearance of a prayer recitation utilizing Talmudic references

1. Harry E. Davis, *A History of Freemasonry Among Negroes in America*, p. 5.
2. Jacob Katz, *Jews and Freemasons in Europe, 1723–1939*. Katz serendipitously happened upon the connection between Jews and Freemasonry that scholars and laypersons alike have shunted as a myth. He was investigating the mobility patterns of Jewish outmigration from the ghetto and began to see the significance of these social ties particularly during the eighteenth and nineteenth centuries. The following section is based primarily upon the historical spadework of Katz.
3. Ibid., p. 203.
4. Ibid., p. 16.

in 1756. Whether the few Jewish members were integrated into the lodges or members of all-Jewish subordinate lodges is unclear. Evidence exists for both interpretations.

The 1780s were a time when the Jewish communities of Europe had reason to hope that all discriminatory restrictions on their civil and social participation would soon be removed. As civil rights were slowly being granted, at least on paper, there was a limited movement of Jews into the mainstream of European society. A small number desired to find a common social framework uniting them with non-Jews who were also educated and liberal in thought. Freemasonry appeared to offer that context. Acceptance into such a Masonic bond had a "twofold significance for the Jew: a sense of personal accomplishment, and the overcoming of the social barrier blocking his group."[5]

But acceptance was not to become a reality. Narrow interpretations began to emerge within Freemasonry stressing the importance of maintaining and nurturing the Christian foundations and requirements of the brotherhood. Much effort appears to have been spent tracing historical roots through medieval Christian orders. One interpretation of this activity could be that this insistence on Christian beliefs was an effort to appease religious opposition. The line of reasoning utilized in the decisionmaking, however, lends support to an interpretation of Jews as beneath the worth of Christians and unacceptable for associational purposes.

Various arguments were advanced as to why Jews should be excluded from the brotherhood. One argument held that such individuals might become marginal to their community if they became Masons and might even be persecuted by their own people.[6] Thus, for their own good they should be excluded. It was also argued that, by the mere action of becoming a Freemason, a Jew would be disrespectful of the religious practices of his people. And if this were so, it constituted evidence of levity toward a matter of grave importance: "In a society such as the Masons, which strove to incorporate within itself the elite

5. Ibid., p. 212.
6. There was a kernel of truth to this rationalization, as there is to most. Some segments of the Jewish community did question the religiosity of those Jews adhering to Masonic beliefs. Jewish conservatism here was similar to the opposition of the Catholic church to the abrogation of rights and duties that were felt to be the responsibility of the religious bodies.

among men, this frivolity and disloyalty would offer sufficient grounds to disqualify an applicant from membership."[7] Others saw admittance of Jews as a major slight to the Christian symbolism inherent in Freemasonry.

> Judaism was presented as a religion of rigid, petrified form, and the Jew as a creature devoid of ethical or brotherly feeling toward any person not of his kind or his community. This stereotype, molded by popular, religious and literary traditions of long standing, had been reinforced by the Jew's appearance, which seemed to set him apart from his fellow man.[8]

Rumors circulated that Jews were attempting to "penetrate, to corrupt, and to make Christian Freemasonry subservient to its [Judaism's] own nefarious purposes."[9] If Jews were not given civil rights, then it was even more dangerous to think of them as being intimate brothers for whom one was responsible. Questions arose repeatedly as to whether Jewish people were fit for membership or whether Jewish Masons from other areas were entitled to visitation rights.

Despite the attacks, some Jewish persons continued to be attracted to the brotherhood, which continued to be perceived as committed to humanistic ideals despite the individual prejudices of a few. The Jewish individual so attracted was persistent:

> He was fully conscious of his similarity to his environment and he fervently believed that the only difference between him and his contemporaries was the allegiance to different religions. Now since religious affiliations were no longer as important as before, his exclusion from the general society constituted no more than senseless discrimination.[10]

7. Katz, *Jews and Freemasons in Europe,* p. 76.
8. Ibid., p. 77.
9. The vehemence of this type of argument can be seen as persisting through the years, although now in aberrant form. A violent diatribe against Jews is found in Erich Ludendorff's pamphlet concerning what he viewed in the early twentieth century as Jewish control and manipulation of Freemasonry for the furtherance of the Jewish world order. Ludendorff, in 1927, contended that Freemasonry had been co-opted by Jews and thus potential leaders of peoples were rendered "innocuous." A disgruntled German Mason who saw himself freeing "judaistically enslaved German Freemasons," Ludendorff saw Judaism permeating all aspects of the doctrine and proceedings of the institution. See *Destruction of Freemasonry Through Revelations of Their Secrets.*
10. Katz, *Jews and Freemasons in Europe,* p. 96.

This paradox within Freemasonry, once recognized by fair-minded individuals, could be relieved by fair treatment, reasoned the Jewish applicant. Discrimination, however, was not easily removed from either public or Masonic affairs. Mainstream lodges continued the pattern of increased rejection of Jews as regular participants or visitors. The struggle to make Freemasonry live up to its ideals was a social struggle to Jews; to non-Jews it was a minor ideological struggle between factions. One document of interesting comparative value is the 1836 petition drafted by Jewish Masons in Hamburg requesting that the Berlin Grand Lodge remove the discriminatory restrictions against Jews. It stated in part:

> We do not appear before you as petitioners begging for favor and mercy, but as relying on the rights which the sanctity of the covenant confers on us . . . Freemasonry calls itself a worldwide covenant; its aim is directed toward spreading the greatest possible unity among mankind—to uproot preconceived ideas, hatred, and strife and to implant love in their place . . . Freemasonry strives for truth. But truth reposes in the human spirit and not in the external forms from which human consideration has found fit to adorn religion . . . [11]

Despite its eloquence, the Berlin lodge was not swayed by the document.

Ironically, a protest was lodged in 1834 by the Grand Lodge of New York, itself a discriminator against black Masons, against the treatment accorded to Jews by the Berlin lodge. The New York lodge, however, backed down after having the local situation explained.[12]

With the Revoluation of 1848, "guardians of the Faith and witchhunters in society turned upon the Freemasons as subverters of the stability of state, society, and Church."[13] The mere fact that the Jewish issue was somehow involved with Freemasonry furthered the spread of conspiracy theories. The link of Freemasons with Jews as undesirable elements emerged around the middle of the nineteenth century in Europe as unrest grew with the rapid erosion of the established patriarchal social order. This was increasingly perceived as the fault of the Jews who were viewed as aggressively greedy in their quest for power. Secret

11. Ibid., p. 98.
12. Ibid., p. 109.
13. Ibid., p. 131.

societies came to be increasingly perceived as a threat in all of western Europe. Contributing to the uneasiness was another trend in the membership of Freemasonry. Catholics were leaving due to threats of excommunication by the Church if they remained. By World War I, conspiracy theories on an international scale abounded, causing an even greater hostility among the Freemasons toward any elements that could further damage their image.

European Masons became more frenetic in their attempt to dissociate themselves from the Jews. Some pamphlets, offered as proof of their loyalty, spoke of how the Masons had systematically kept Jews out of the lodges. Others mentioned the small number of Jewish members and their restriction to lower positions in the lodges. Not many were convinced:

> If the Masons expected to appease their adversaries by yielding, they were mistaken. Once the propagandists had begun their attack on Jews and Freemasons in the same breath, the patriotism of the Freemasons was no longer taken for granted. While the Freemasons dissociated themselves from the Jews, other circles sought to dissociate themselves from the Freemasons.[14]

Masons in the Prussian militia were one such group. Public propaganda increased with the Masons now "exposed to public gaze as an exclusive and arrogant minority, which, like the Jews, did not acknowledge the slightest brotherly obligation to any but their own."[15] In 1933, the Nazis ordered the dissolution of Masonic lodges.

The Jewish experience with Masonry in America has been minimized by the availability of alternative contexts and organizational forms, but discrimination against Jews has occurred throughout the country.[16] Whether in Europe or America, the Jewish Mason remained like the black Mason: a marginal man

14. Ibid., p. 191.
15. Ibid., p. 192.
16. By the time large numbers of Jews were living in the United States, B'nai B'rith chapters of the international fraternity were well established in the States. It is important that the first B'nai B'rith chapter in Europe was founded in Germany by ex-Masons who had resigned because of the overt anti-Semitism of the members. Some Jewish Freemasons objected to the rapid spread of the Jewish organization, seeing it as capitulation to the discriminatory practices of mainstream Freemasonry. See Katz, *Jews and Freemasons in Europe*, p. 165.

rejected by barriers to recognition of his individual achievement.

Another situation of Freemason discrimination involved the Mormons. The first Mormon Masonic organization was formed in 1842.[17] Mainstream Masonry, however, did not recognize the group as legitimate, claiming procedural difficulties in the manner the group was constituted and its members selected. The situation is complicated by charges from mainstream Masons that portions of the Masonic ritual had been stolen for use in the Mormon Temple ceremonies. The Mormon religious ceremonies and those of Freemasonry share the following: five points of fellowship; oaths with similar penalties; gestures such as thumb signal across the throat as an indication of penalty; secret grip and password sequence; similar signs; similar apron attire for hierarchical degrees; the square and compass as important symbolic referents; procedures virtually identical step by step.[18] The similarities are indeed striking. Of particular interest is the history of the Mormon experience of acceptance and rejection by the mainstream body.

It is well known that Mormons, in their various settlements, experienced problems with the established powers in an area. This is reflected in their Freemasonry. The Mormon Masonic organizations that were established were investigated by mainstream bodies, who tended to deny or revoke their char-

17. Special appreciation is here given to Roy Canning, University of Utah, who first called my attention to the many parallels between Masonry and Mormonism.

18. See Jerald Tanner and Sandra Tanner, *Mormonism: Shadow or Reality?* They contend that passages in twenty-one chapters in seven out of sixteen books in the Book of Mormon refer to Masonry. They allege the parallel to be more than the similarity in usage of secrecy. The Gadiantons, prominent in the Book of Mormon, are said to directly parallel Masons. See also J. H. Adamson, "The Treasure of the Widow's Son." The similarity in ritual and penalties is striking. In 1931, one Temple oath read that "if one revealed any of the secrets one knew" that "our throats be cut from ear to ear and our tongues torn out by their roots!" This has been modified now to the pledge that rather than violating the secret the Mormon "would suffer my life to be taken." The similarity to the Masonic second-degree oath is evident. That oath in 1931 read that the penalty for violation was "to have our breasts cut open and our hearts and vitals torn free from our bodies and given to the air and the beasts of the field." See Tanner and Tanner, *Mormonism*, p. 474.

ters. They were declared clandestine (bogus) by bodies such as the Grand Lodge of Illinois. Various reasons were cited: failure to pay dues regularly and properly, irregular practices from a lack of thorough preparatory work, incorrect forms of procedure, nonadherence to age and sex regulations, improper submission of records, and their belief in plural gods.

But the Mormon Masonic lodges continued to function. Many of the converts to Mormonism were already Masons. One convincing reason for joining the fellowship was that Brigham Young was a Mason. However, the political implications should be considered, for they are crucial to an understanding of the relationship between Freemasonry and Mormons.

The state politicians in Illinois, and later Utah, were particularly interested in those individuals who could possibly deliver the Mormon vote when needed. Both the Whigs and the Democrats, almost evenly balanced in Illinois, courted the Mormon leaders, who in turn bathed in the unusual experience of power. Stephen A. Douglas, then Illinois secretary of state, used his influence to expedite matters for various Mormon lodges. He and other individual politicians could rationalize that both Masons and Mormons were emphasizing appreciation of culture and ancient arts. As the importance of the Mormon vote lessened, the attack on Mormon Masons—never accepted on a formal basis by mainstream Freemasonry—increased.

Native Americans have also had experience with mainstream Freemasonry. Some Indian leaders were initiated into Freemasonry in the late eighteenth and early nineteenth centuries. Many of these were individuals who traveled east on tribal business with the federal government or who dealt with traders and westward travelers. It is likely that the occasions for initiation were incidences of benefits for mainstream members.

A regular lodge of Cherokees (Cherokee Lodge No. 21) is listed in 1848 in Oklahoma, chartered by the Grand Lodge of Arkansas.[19] One history, written by a Mason, offers the explanation that many "found in Freemasonry a teaching and a way of life which fitted their philosophies far better than any of the numerous sectarian doctrines of devouted missionaries."[20]

19. William R. Denslow, *Freemasonry and the American Indian,* p. 37.
20. Ibid., p. iv. Denslow discusses similarities between Indian and Masonic signs. For example, Denslow states that each Indian tribe had a distinguishing sign by which one could identify and place the other. The

But Native Americans were not considered worthy of the brotherhood by most mainstream Masons. In the nineteenth century there was increased opposition to the initiation into regular, or even separate, lodges since the Native Americans came to be defined as "too illiterate and debased in morals, habits and religion to allow them of being worthy and creditable members."[21] Brotherly responsibility could not be extended to such persons.

There is some evidence that upwardly mobile Chinese individuals also sought membership in Masonic lodges.[22] While one-way visitation occurred occasionally, Chinese Freemasonry was always a separate entity, considered irregular and not granted full recognition.

Having noted the similarities in other experiences, we turn again to particular aspects of the black experience. The irregular status of black Freemasonry has been an emotionally charged issue, and various arguments have been presented and refuted on the legitimacy of the separate black body.

It has been argued by persons in opposition to Prince Hall Freemasonry that new lodges cannot be created within a geographical area already having a lodge. From this it is held that the original intitiation of fifteen black Freemasons by the Irish lodge was irregular and that the separate lodge established after the military lodge left the area had no legitimacy.

Prince Hall Masons disagree and state that their origins in the Irish military lodge are indeed valid. Even if the argument of the invasion of established territory held, they maintain, the only restriction would have been that such a military lodge initiation could not have occurred if there were another Irish lodge in town, which was not the case in Massachusetts at the time. Thus, in the context of the time and circumstances, the initiation of blacks was a legitimate act.[23]

Cheyenne, for example, drew the lower edge of the right hand across the left arm (as if gashing if with a knife). He notes the parallel to a similar Masonic gesture.

21. *National Fraternal Review*, May 1928, p. 2.

22. See Stanford M. Lyman, "Chinese Secret Societies in the Occident: Notes and Suggestions for Research in the Sociology of Secrecy," *Canadian Review of Sociology and Anthropology,* pp. 79–102.

23. Harry A. Williamson, "Legitimacy of Negro Masonry," *National Fraternal Review,* May 1924, p. 4. He cites examples of white dual territorial jurisdiction in New York, Pennsylvania, Virginia, and other states.

The doctrine of in-context validation allows for the fact that several mainstream lodges owe their existence to similar processes by military lodges of Irish, English, and Scottish constitutions. Union Lodge of Albany—now Mt. Vernon Lodge No. 3—was born in New York during the same period as the original African lodge.[24] Black Masons argue that dispute over this matter is spurious since few grand lodges were in existence in 1775. They point out that in 1791 only eleven grand lodges existed in the entire western hemisphere. As one black Mason wrote: "It is pertinent to note here that African Lodge was openly and publicly established at a time when there were numerous white lodges in Boston and New England. No protests against this establishment were filed with England, nor was its legitimacy ever assailed by the Masons of that time, nor was invasion of jurisdiction asserted."[25]

Questions have also been raised about the length of time between the admission of the fifteen blacks by the military lodge and the obtaining of the charter for the separate African lodge from the Mother Lodge. Prince Hall Freemasons counter that many mainstream lodges existed in acceptable form for even longer periods. The circumstances of the extended period, moreover, have nothing to do with questions by the Mother Lodge about the charter for the black body. Aside from the formidable deterrent of the Revolutionary War, there was a mix-up of sailing ships, messages, and deliveries by captains. The request for a charter had been accepted and was finally delivered on 19 April 1787 to Prince Hall by Captain Scott, a sailing master and brother-in-law of John Hancock.[26]

Another charge that has been repeatedly advanced against the black organization has been that African Lodge No. 459 was not included under the wing of the 1792 Grand Lodge of Massachusetts. Prince Hall Masons offer several plausible explanations for the exclusion. While it may have been a discriminatory exclusion, it may also have been, as in the case of many lodges,

24. Traveling warrants were begun by the Ireland Grand Lodge in 1732 and were generally accepted. See Frank H. Hankins, "Masonry," *Encyclopedia of the Social Sciences,* p. 179.
25. Harry E. Davis, "Documents Relating to Negro Masonry in America," *Journal of Negro History,* p. 430.
26. Ibid., p. 418.

that the black body chose not to affiliate.[27] Further, few Masons of that time paid much attention to principles of formal organization. Given the temper of the times, such regulations could have easily been overlooked or discounted.

It appears that there was general indifference among early mainstream Boston Masons to the African lodge. By 1779 there were at least thirty-four members in the Boston black lodge,[28] a sizable number to overlook. A letter from Prince Hall to the local newspaper in the winter of 1782 also supports indifference toward the black group.[29] Prince Hall informed the paper of a mistake in its identification of the black body. Noting that the group had celebrated the Feast of St. John's, a Masonic ritual, the paper identified the Masons as "St. Black's Lodge." Hall acknowledged, with suitable eighteenth-century propriety, that the paper might have meant the label to be a candid description, but suggests that such a label violates the Masonic spirit of universal love.[30] Black Masons were visible in Boston, for in 1784 Henry Rose issued permission to the black body to practice Masonic burial and parade procedures.

Black Masons also mention that Prince Hall was the only American Masonic correspondent to the Masonic headquarters in Great Britain after 1775. In 1792, the year when the Grand Lodge of Massachusetts was established, Hall was asked by the Mother Lodge in England to check on the existence of various white lodges that were not responding to correspondence.[31] This clearly shows the esteem of the black leader and organization, according to the Prince Hall Masons.

There is also a charge against the black body based on the omission of a listing of the Prince Hall body by the Mother Lodge of England. The nineteenth-century document purports

27. Williamson believes that the African lodge did apply but was refused recognition as a duly and regularly constituted lodge for discriminatory reasons. See Williamson, "Legitimacy of Negro Masonry," *National Fraternal Review*, p. 3.

28. See Harold Van Buren Voorhis, *Negro Masonry in the United States*, p. 16.

29. One excellent source of information concerning this period is Prince Hall's Letter Book, now in run-down condition but intact. The book, presently in the archives of the Prince Hall Grand Lodge of Massachusetts, contains sermons and correspondence for the period 1782 through 1806.

30. See Davis, *History of Freemasonry*, p. 413.

31. Voorhis, *Negro Masonry*, p. 29.

to be a complete listing of worldwide Masonry. This argument is countered by evidence that the mainstream Boston lodge was also omitted, yet the Boston lodge is traditionally venerated as the oldest (1733) continuous American lodge.[32] Those arguing for the continuous good standing of Prince Hall Freemasonry cite the general confusion between the colonies and Great Britain around the time of the Revolutionary War. Not only was the African lodge erased from the rolls, but so was any lodge that had not contributed at that time to the England Grand Charity Fund.

Further confusion stems from a major breach within universal Freemasonry from which the two factions of the body stem: those of Ancient and those of Modern descent. When the rivalry between the Ancient and Modern lodges was healed in the new nation, the African Grand Lodge, duly descended from the Mother Grand Lodge of England, was not included on lists printed by the mainstream body.

The specification in the Ancient charges that all Masonic candidates be freeborn is at the center of one particular attack on black Freemasonry. It is said that the black brotherhood has not always followed this stricture. The issue of freeborn status as a Masonic requirement was discussed and modified at one point within universal Masonry. In 1847, a West Indian grand lodge spoke of the issue raised by the abolition of slavery by Parliament. The grand master urged all brethren to change the requirement to "free agent" rather than "free born." In response, the Grand Lodge of England changed the constitution to read "free man"; the Canadian and Australian lodges did likewise. The white American lodges did not follow suit, however.[33]

Prince Hall Freemasonry intially held to the old constitutional requirement that a member must be freeborn, a requirement originally incorporated into Freemasonry because of the nature of the solemn contract involved:

> No one can legally bind himself to its performance who is not a free agent and the master of his own actions. . . . Birth in a service condition is accompanied by a degradation of mind and

32. Grand Lodge of Massachusetts, 1947; Davis, *History of Freemasonry,* p. 189; Harry A. Williamson, "Prince Hall or Negro Masonry," *The Masonic Analyst.*
33. William H. Grimshaw, *Official History of Freemasonry Among the Colored People in North America,* p. 42.

abasement of spirit which no subsequent disentralment can so completely efface as to render the party qualified to perform his duties, as a Mason, with that "freedom, fervency and zeal" which is said to have distinguished our ancient brethren.[34]

While the original Prince Hall Masons were certainly free blacks, it is highly unlikely that all of the early Masons were freeborn, although this is the contention held until emancipation. This is not considered problematic by Prince Hall practitioners. Martin Delany, a black physician and noted leader and spokesman of his time, wrote in 1853 of the irony of holding to the freeborn convention:

> In many parts of the world the people of avaricious nations were subject to lose their liberty in several ways: A forfeiture by crime, as in our country; by voluntary servitude for a stipulated sum or reward, as among the Hindoos [*sic*]; and by capture in battle and being sold into slavery, as in Algiers. . . . As there must be criminal intention in the commission of a crime, so must the act of the criminal be voluntary; hence the criminal and the voluntary bondsman have both forfeited their Masonic rights by willing degradation. In the case of a captive, an entirely different person is presented before us, who has greater claims upon our sympathies than the untrammeled freeman. Instead of the degraded vassal and voluntary slave, whose prostrate position only facilitates the aspect of his horrible deformity, you have the bold, the brave, the high-minded, the independent spirited and manly form of a kindred brother in humanity, whose heart is burning, whose breast is heaving, and whose soul is wrung with panting aspirations for liberty. . . . Does Masonry, then, contemplate the withholding of its applicants as these? Certainly not; since Moses (to whom our great Grand Master Solomon, the founder of the temple, is indebted for his Masonic wisdom) was born, and lived in captivity eighty years, and was by the laws of his captors a slave. It matters not whether captured in actual conflict, sleeping by the wayside, or in liberty and a manly determination to be free. Policy alone will not permit the order to confer Masonic privileges on one while yet in captivity; but the fact of his former condition as such, or that of his parents, can have no bearing on him.[35]

The contention that blacks could not truly function as Freema-

34. Albert G. Mackey, *Encyclopedia of Freemasonry and Kindred Sciences*, p. 295.

35. Quoted in Silas H. Shephard, "An Invaluable Bibliography: Notes on the Literature Dealing with Negro Freemasonry," *National Trestle Board*, p. 29.

sons due to previous condition of servitude is neatly refuted. The appeal to Moses did not, however, erase the colorphobia of white mainstream Masonry.

Mainstream Masons have not intitiated court proceedings against Prince Hall Masonic operations—as they have against groups they believe to be clandestine or irregular (not following organizational rules and procedures)—which is cited as de facto proof of their latent acknowledgment of the legitimacy of black Freemasonry. Supporting this are joint collaborations between black and white lodges in actions against groups deemed as Masonic imposters. Officials of white organizations have joined with black officials to prosecute clandestine black groups.

In 1818, the mainstream grand lodge appointed a committee to investigate black Freemasonry after a newspaper advertisement appeared calling for a meeting of the members of the African lodge. This appears to have been the first inquiry into the regularity of the black organization. The committee reported that the body was clandestine, but no court action was taken.[36]

In 1827, the Prince Hall body published a statement of policy in a Boston newspaper that stated that the lodge members "declared themselves free and independent of any Lodge from this day and that we will not be tributary or be governed by any Lodges than that of our own."[37] The impetus for this pronouncement is not known, however.

White lodges occasionally pondered the question of the fitness of blacks for the craft. A New York lodge, in 1851, decided that it was not "proper" to "initiate Negroes in accordance with Masonic law and their Ancient charges and regulations, because of their depressed social conditions, their general lack of intelligence, which unfits them, as a body, to work in or adorn the craft; the impropriety in making them our equals in one place, when from their social condition and circumstances which almost everywhere attach to them," the situation is hopeless. The statement continues about the inability of blacks to trace their lineage and existence to honest livelihoods. This lodge also warned of the problem that might arise in the future as to the

36. Voorhis, *Negro Masonry*, p. 43; Harvey N. Brown, *Freemasonry Among Negroes and Whites in America*, p. 30.
37. Voorhis, *Negro Masonry*, p. 38. In 1875, the white Grand Lodge of Ohio discussed the matter without taking any action. Ibid., p. 44.

higher degree of intellectual fitness that some blacks might have as a result of the "admixtures of white blood."[38]

A formal petition by seventy-two black Masons from five lodges was presented to the Grand Lodge of Massachusetts in 1868, asking official Masonic recognition of the equal standing of Prince Hall Freemasonry.[39] This was not the first such request. It did not suggest integration of the parallel organization, only legitimacy in the eyes of the white body. A committee was appointed to review the matter. After a preliminary investigation, it recommended that the petiton be withdrawn.[40]

The Washington (State) Grand Lodge acknowledged the existence of Prince Hall lodges within the state in 1898, leaving the matter of relations among subordinate lodges to their own discretion. Several subordinate lodges severed their connections in protest over this limited recognition of blacks.[41] One Washington Mason was so intrigued by his review of the history of the black organization that he inserted a provision in his will "that no monument be erected over [my] grave until both white and colored Masons could stand beside it as brothers in the fullest sense of the word."[42]

Other individual white Masons spoke with praise of black Freemasons:

> If brethren would read some of the splendid orations that have been delivered by negro Masons these might tend to give them a better conception of a race which has progressed with remarkable rapidity when we stop to consider the handicaps which they have been subject to, the mistreatment they have undergone and the prejudice which even men who have taken the degree of Masonry sometimes feel toward them. It would appear from everything which is said about Prince Hall Masons that they represent the best element of their people.[43]

The schizophrenic nature of white confusion over Prince Hall Freemasonry can be seen by the actions of Albert Pike, a Mason

---

38. Williamson, *Freemasonry Among the American Negroes*, p. 9.

39. Lewis Hayden, "Masonry Among Colored Men in Massachusetts," p. 43.

40. Davis, "Documents Relating to Negro Masonry," *Journal of Negro History*, chapter twelve.

41. Voorhis, *Negro Masonry in the United States*, p. 44.

42. Davis, *History of Freemasonry*, p. 158.

43. Silas H. Shepard, "An Invaluable Bibliography," *National Trestle Board*, p. 29.

himself and one of the most noted historians of Masonry. A rabid "Negrophobe," Pike stated repeatedly that he would renounce Masonry before he would recognize a black Mason as a brother. He did not wish to be "contaminated by the leprosy of Negro association."[44] Yet when Pike published a massive work on the Scottish Rite, he gave a complete set to the Prince Hall Southern Jurisdiction Sovereign Grand Commander. It appears that Pike, as others, feared that formal Masonic recognition would lead to the absorption of black Masons. Instead, he was willing to let the craft function independently.

Black Masons have acknowledged the accolades from individual white Masons for their "achievement in the face of such a solid phalanx of opposition and discouragement."[45] Harry A. Williamson's *A History of Freemasonry Among American Negroes,* published in 1929, carries in the preface his acknowledgement of thanks to "two Caucasian Masons (whose identities, for obvious reasons, cannot be revealed at this time)." Interestingly, the foreword is by a white British Mason.

The issue of the function of separate organizations came up again in 1924 when the Supreme Council, Northern Jurisdiction, was forced to consider the matter of black Freemasonry in the settlement of a legal matter. The circumstance was the existence of black Scottish Rite Masons in New Jersey having the same name for their supreme council as that of the white Masonic body. There had been no complaint until the black organization purchased land and constructed a magnificent edifice on valuable property. When incorporation became necessary for the conduct of the business enterprise, the similarities in name became problematic. The white supreme council extended an offer of informal cooperation to the black United Supreme Council. Official Masonic recognition was not adopted, but the white body acknowledged the black group (after the latter had changed its name) as being within the tradition of universal Freemasonry.[46]

The matter does not appear in the records again until the 1940s when the Grand Lodge of Massachusetts unanimously accepted the 1947 report of an appointed committee investigat-

44. Davis, *History of Freemasonry,* p. 26.
45. See Williamson, *Freemasonry Among the American Negroes.*
46. Davis, "Documents Relating to Negro Masonry," *Journal of Negro History,* pp. 249– 50; Davis, *History of Freemasonry,* pp. 28– 29.

ing the status of the Prince Hall body. A large-scale investigation had been conducted, the first in over fifty years and the first ever to go beyond consideration of technical irregularities. One of the committee members was Dr. Melvin M. Johnson, a former dean of the Boston University Law School. Johnson said that he had begun the exhaustive study with the goal of proving the illegitimacy of the black group, but became convinced that the Prince Hall Masons were the only lodge in America possessing an original charter granted by the Mother Grand Lodge of England.[47]

The committee recognized the body's adherence to Masonic practices and procedures in Massachusetts and urged that descent from the Mother Grand Lodge of England be recognized by all white Masons. The committee, however, was split over the potential controversy. The report concluded that "in view of the existing social conditions in our country, it is advisable for the official and organized activities of white and colored Freemasons to proceed in parallel lines, but organically separate and without mutually embarrassing demands or commitments . . . within these limitations, informal cooperation and mutual helpfulness between the two groups upon appropriate occasions are desirable."[48]

Having acknowledged the Prince Hall organization as legitimate and duly constituted, the dangers of social intermingling and the embarrassment of mutual responsibilities are recognized as paramount. But even this limited action caused a reactionary response. Under pressure from other state grand lodges, the Grand Lodge of Massachusetts unanimously rescinded its original action two years later.[49]

Some white Masons did speak up against the rescindment, calling it sheer cowardice:

> Massachusetts Masonry was not only "stupid," but worse; it did not have the moral courage to live up to that which it knew in its heart was right. It has been said that it is infinitely more corrupt

47. "Masonic Report Upholds 'Prince Hall Affiliation,'" *Christian Science Monitor*, 13 March 1947.

48. Ibid.; Voorhis, *Negro Masonry*, p. 45; "Segregation in Brotherhood," *Negro History Bulletin*.

49. The grand lodges in Georgia, Texas, Alabama, and Florida were prime movers here. See Brown, *Freemasonry Among Negroes and Whites in America*, pp. 11, 59.

to refuse to do that which is known to be right than to do wrong because of inferiority and ignorance, which might describe roughly the position of Massachusetts vis-à-vis North Carolina and other Grand Lodges of a similar outlook. Boston, the "Athens of America," has no excuse; perhaps North Carolina does. The Grand Lodge of Massachusetts has compromised its own honor. Only its own Brethren can restore that honor, by calmly and fearlessly admitting their error, and reconsidering their position. Then, and not until then, will Massachusetts Freemasonry once again occupy its rightful position, without the necessity for apology, as the first official Freemasonry in America, and the most influencial.[50]

This opinion, however, was clearly not that of the majority, and the dilemma still exists.

Many white Freemasons have remained oblivious to the racial paradox within their midst.[51] Some have even actively opposed the civil rights activities of the last two decades:

> One might suspect that the "spiritual home" of many Southern Masons (and some Northern, too) is in the Klan rather than in the Masonic Fraternity. It would not be amiss to point out that of the three Southern leaders, all whom took a part in the struggle against equal rights for our Negro citizens, were Governors Wallace and Faubus, of Alabama and Arkansas respectively, and former Governor Ross Barnet of Mississippi: all were Freemasons.[52]

The tie between white Masonry and the Ku Klux Klan must be mentioned. Reverend Simmons, the revitalizer of the Klan in its second rebirth, was active in Masonry and several other fraternal orders. David Chalmers's state-by-state analysis of the Klan cites advertisements in some areas that solicited members by stating that Masons were preferred. Chalmers found that Masons were often sought to sell the Klan's brand of fraternalism "since they [were] likely to be skilled in the world of ritualism and fraternal dynamics." Masons as a whole were ambivalent, but many thousands of the rank and file, particularly from the Scottish Rite and Organe lodges, became Klansmen.[53]

50. Ibid., p. 91.
51. Alvin J. Schmidt and Nicholas Babchuk, "The Unholy Brotherhood: Discrimination in Fraternal Orders," *Phylon.*
52. Brown, *Freemasonry*, p. 76.
53. David M. Chalmers, *Hooded Americanism: The First Century of the Ku Klux Klan, 1865–1965;* see also Loretta J. Williams, "The Social Psychology of Secret Societies."

In 1970, the Massachusetts grand lodge again acknowledged that the Prince Hall body was functioning on all levels and degrees in a duly constituted manner. This was after an open letter signed by twenty white Massachusetts Masons was sent to the grand lodge asking why nothing had been done in the twenty-odd years since the body had declared Prince Hall Freemasonry as regular and legitimate.[54] Again, resolution of the issue was sidestepped.

54. Among the signers were Edwin Canham, editor of *The Christian Science Monitor;* and Kivie Kaplan, then national president of the National Association for the Advancement of Colored People.

Chapter 8

Black Association:
Pragmatic Adaptation?

Black fraternal organizations, including Prince Hall Free-masonry, are a major vehicle for social integration and inter-course within black society. Enjoying considerable community prestige, these nationwide associations have major importance for their members and the communities in which they reside.[1] While the major focus is upon black Freemasonry, it is useful to examine the associational context of the black community. How usual or unusual is it for blacks to belong to an organization such as Prince Hall Freemasonry?

Black communities have supported a variety of forms of social and civic associations. In the early periods, burial societies were abundant, attracting individuals, usually of rural background, anxious to prepare for their demise so as to not financially burden their kinfolk. This phenomenon is not peculiar to blacks; it is instead a phenomenon of class. Benevolent societies were also of major importance in the early black communities and remained prevalent until large-scale insurance companies developed. Many of these were secret societies for mutual aid; others were more business-oriented. Now extinct, one of the largest business-oriented societies was the Grand United Order of True Reformers. Of this group, founded by an ex-slave from Georgia, Charles Wesley has written: "This organization de-veloped into one of the most important groups from the point of view of resources and membership then existing in the United States. Its business organization marked one of the epochs in the development of Negro business."[2] It is unfortunate that few written records of these organizations exist. There have been,

1. Howard W. Odum found in 1910 that there was less rivalry among black lodges and societies than among black churches. The same findings might occur today. See *Social and Mental Traits of the Negro*.
2. Charles H. Wesley, *History of the Improved Benevolent and Protective*

however, an abundance of secret societies within the black community for which we do have records: Odd Fellows, Elks, Colored Knights of Pythias, Grand Order of True Reformers, and the Knights of Tabor are the foremost.[3]

Some formed as exclusive organizations. In Charleston, South Carolina, for example, there was a society formed in the 1790s of light-skinned West Indian emigrés called the Brown Fellowship Society. This benevolent association was "open to free brown men only and a symbol of mulatto exclusiveness."[4] Four fraternal organizations are known to have existed in geographically dispersed communities before the Civil War: Prince Hall Freemasons, Odd Fellows, Galilean Fishermen, and the Nazarites. All members were free blacks at that time. But other organizations crossed class lines, such as the United Brothers of Friendship and Sisters of the Mysterious Ten, established in Louisville in the mid-nineteenth century. Both free blacks and slaves were members, suggesting a lowered degree of class antagonism. This organization is said to have had 100,000 members by 1892.[5]

The major organizations—those not confined to a particular city or town—were most often emulations of institutions found within the dominant society. Some black organizations, by white default, emerged from formerly white organizations by an invasion process. In the 1870s there was a secret society promoting charity and temperance called the Independent Order of Good Samaritans and Daughters of Samaria. Initially it was an all-white organization; blacks came to be accepted to the order but were not allowed to meet with or preside over whites. Separate subordinate branches were established with the black branches

Order of Elks of the World 1898–1954, p. 22. Unfortunately, no detailed analysis of this group appears to have been conducted. There undoubtedly would be difficulty in finding and obtaining any records.

3. Frank L. Mather in *Who's Who of the Colored Race,* published to celebrate a half-century of freedom for blacks in the United States, notes with pride the abundance of black fraternal organizations. Within that volume are listed: Galilean Fishermen, National Ideal Benefit Association, Grand United Order of Wise Men and Women, United Order of Good Shepherd, Grand United Order of Tents of the J. R. Giddings and Jollifee Union, Grand United Order of the Sons and Daughters of Peace, and the Royal Circle of Friends of the World.

4. Ira Berlin, *Slaves Without Masters: The Free Negro in the Antebellum South,* p. 58.

5. Charles W. Ferguson, *Fifty Million Brothers.*

having limited representation in the general assemblies. The group, however, became all-black when the white members withdrew as larger numbers of blacks became members.

There were other contexts for emergence. A petition by free blacks to the American Odd Fellows in 1842, asking for a dispensation for an all-black lodge, was refused. However, Peter Ogden, a black Odd Fellow initiated into an English lodge, was pivotal in the establishment of the first black lodge: Philomathean No. 646 of New York. No evidence exists that blacks ever petitioned for regular admittance to the order once they were established as a separate body.[6]

The Improved Benevolent Order of Elks of the World (the black parallel organization) was founded in Cincinnati in 1898 after entrance had been denied into the white organization.[7] This organization has been the closest in appeal to Prince Hall Freemasonry. Mainstream American Elkdom emerged from a small group of actors, The Jolly Corks, who began meeting for social and recreational purposes in 1867.[8] Gradually, rituals for new members, usually actors or literary men, began to develop with ways to instantly recognize a brother from a group of strangers. As the group continued to develop and codify its requirements, a white-only clause was inserted that was inconsistent with its stated intention to encourage "manly fellowship and kindly intercourse."[9] It is likely that there were black members prior to the 1890 clause. Light-complexioned blacks interested in the theater were forced to "pass" in order to follow their professional inclinations. Further, the 1900 census listed 2,043 black actors, so it is quite likely that there were early black Odd Fellows.[10]

The parallel black structure was established by Arthur J. Riggs, a Pullman porter with easy access to the ritual and workings of the fellowship. Charles Wesley writes:

> Whether Riggs secured an Elk Ritual by gift, or by one being

6. Edward N. Palmer, "Negro Secret Societies," *Social Forces,* p. 209.
7. Marcus Boulware, *The Oratory of Negro Leaders 1900–1968.*
8. Corks was a bar game popular in that period. There was no organized baseball, football, or basketball at this time. See Wesley, *Improved Benevolent,* for a more extensive description and analysis.
9. Ibid., p. 33.
10. Ibid., p. 35.

left inadvertently on his train, or in an office, or elsewhere, cannot be ascertained as Riggs did not reveal his method of obtaining it. The traditions of the pullman service were of such high caliber and the integrity of Riggs was such that it seems that the stealing of it was beyond the realm of probability, although it was entirely possible.[11]

Riggs lost his job once it was officially known by white Elks that he had formed a duplicate structure for black persons. The organization was challenged by whites but the black members had copyrighted the ritual, which the white Elks had not. The black organization grew rapidly with its greatest appeal in the urban settings where parades, military drills, and scholarship programs drew public attention to the organization. In general, the Elks are more secular in outlook and more admittedly social than Freemasons.[12]

Other racially pillarized responses to discriminatory treatment are Greek-letter sororities and fraternities. Their beginnings are more recent, which is not surprising given the late arrival of blacks in institutions of higher learning in sufficient numbers to support black organizations. The first such fraternity was Alpha Phi Alpha, founded in 1905 by several black students at Cornell University who banded together to form the initial chapter in response to feelings of isolation on the campus.[13]

The University of Indiana was the site of the founding of Kappa Alpha Psi in 1911, and Howard University the setting for the emergence of Alpha Kappa Alpha, a black sorority. Omega Psi Phi, Phi Beta Sigma, and Delta Sigma Theta (sorority) were also founded at Howard University. All have grown to have a national staff and nationwide membership. The fact that several of the fraternities and sororities emerged in segregated settings indicates that isolation was not the sole or crucial factor. All of

11. Ibid., p. 42.
12. See E. Franklin Frazier, "Recreation and Amusement Among American Negroes." Frazier states that Masonic lodges appeal more to rural-minded people while Elks appeal to more urban-minded persons. While this question was not incorporated into the current research, Frazier's conclusion seems impressionistic and not supported by existent data.
13. Richard T. Watkins, "Black Social Order: Expanding Their Goals to Fit the Needs of the Community at Large," *Black Enterprise,* pp. 26–29; see also the works of Charles H. Wesley for extensive documentation on black fraternities.

the organizations have fostered expertise in leadership as well as self-expression. All have met preceived needs for social recognition within the black community.

Gunnar Myrdal, in his classic *An American Dilemma,* utilized the research findings of E. Franklin Frazier to pronounce these black associations as outstanding features of the black community. Myrdal speaks of the black associations as recreational outlets for the establishment and maintenance of a high evaluation.[14]

Voluntary associations exemplify the principle of freedom of association conjoined with that of common interest.[15] Social scientists view such associations as an opportunity to illuminate the relationship between individual needs and societal requirements. The literature on voluntary associations, although replete with contradictory findings, would suggest that black organizations assist in easing the strains inherent in a discriminatory social system. They facilitate adjustment, operating as a social mechanism buffering or bridging the gap between the practices of major societal institutions and their stated ideals.[16] The multiplicity of organizations within the black community has been interpreted as compensation for restrictions upon social participation in society.[17]

There is a debate concerning majority versus minority propensity toward voluntary associational affiliation. Some argue that whites are more apt to join voluntary associations than blacks.[18] However, the greater weight of the evidence points in

14. Gunnar Myrdal, *An American Dilemma.*

15. David Sills, "Voluntary Associations: Sociological Aspects," *International Encyclopedia Social Sciences,* pp. 362–79.

16. Sherwood Fox, "Voluntary Associations and Social Structure," Ph.D. diss., Harvard University, classified voluntary associations into three types: majoral, including business and professional organizations serving, or in auxiliary relation to, the major institutions of society; minoral, including religious and ethnic associations that serve the interests of significant minorities within the system; medial associations such as social service organizations that mediate between the various segments of the society.

17. Guy B. Johnson, "Some Factors in the Development of Negro Social Institutions in the United States," *American Journal of Sociology,* pp. 329–37.

18. See Sills, *Voluntary Associations;* Charles R. Wright and Herbert Hyman, "Voluntary Association Membership of American Adults: Evidence from National Sample Surveys," *American Sociological Review,* pp. 284–94.

the other direction.[19] Gunnar Myrdal's study of black-white relations in the 1930s and 1940s documented the greater number of associational forms in the black community and that there was a greater likelihood of a black belonging to a voluntary association than a white. Myrdal described blacks as "exaggerated Americans." He was particularly cognizant of the impact of the church and voluntary associatons. Similarly, St. Clair Drake and Horace Cayton saw a multiplicity of black organizations in their study of Chicago's black community of the 1930s. They suggested a trend: the black lower class tended to join voluntary associations revolving around the black church while the black middle class tended toward associational forms patterned after those of the dominant society.[20] A later study by Anthony Orum, reviewing and evaluating previous findings, found that class was not a reliable predictor of black social participation.[21] His findings add credence to the arguments that community social mobility patterns and attitudes are significantly related to associational membership.[22]

Other studies have also attempted to interpret the associational involvement of blacks. A community study in Lincoln, Nebraska, concluded that blacks participate more often and more actively than whites. This greater participation was interpreted as evidence of alternative avenues for achievement and status recognition for blacks.[23] Others have expanded the discussion to the functional pragmatism motivating associational participation. Marvin Olsen, for example, rejects the tradition-

19. Chicago Commission on Race Relations, *The Negro in Chicago: A Study of Race Relations and a Race Riot;* Carter G. Woodson, *The Negro Professional Man;* Myrdal, *An American Dilemma.* An astute observation on associational affiliation is given by Max Lerner in *America as a Civilization.* Lerner ponders the professional academic's disdain for joiners. He spoofs academics for overlooking their own multiple associations when they downgrade Americans for being overly involved.
20. St. Clair Drake and Horace Cayton, *Black Metropolis.*
21. Anthony Orum, "A Reappraisal of the Social and Political Participation of Negroes," *American Journal of Sociology,* pp. 32–46.
22. Howard E. Freeman, Edwin Nowak, and Leo G. Reeder, "Correlates of Membership in Voluntary Associations," *American Sociological Review,* pp. 528–33.
23. Nicholas Babchuk and Ralph V. Thompson, "The Voluntary Association of Negroes," *American Sociological Review,* pp. 647–55; see also Edyth L. Ross, *Black Heritage in Social Welfare: 1860–1930.*

ally accepted compensation thesis and offers instead an ethnic-community thesis that "blacks who identify as members of an ethnic minority tend to be more active than nonidentifiers."[24]

Some have questioned the involvement of blacks in such a plethora of organizations, seeing such forms as escapist and diversionary from continuous efforts for change. Often such discussions of black associations have failed to examine the variety of types of associations in black circles. Factors such as historical period, region, objectives, and context must be considered prior to generalizations. Burial societies are quite different from fraternal organizations, as are the numerous benevolent societies that declined with the growth of black insurance companies. More concern has been expressed over black fraternities and secret societies. Both Myrdal and Frazier viewed black fraternities as minimal in importance and unnecessarily imitative in form,[25] an evaluation that can be challenged. Both saw blacks attempting to mirror activities of true Americana. Some black clergymen, particularly in the nineteenth century, were enraged by the greater loyalty expressed by their parishioners to their fraternal lodges. Publisher and orator Frederick Douglass chided blacks in fraternities for time spent in rituals of secrecy rather than actions for change.[26] The concerns of the ministers and spokespersons raise questions of the interpretations of Myrdal and Frazier, and, more recently, William A. Muraskin, who views black Freemasonry as an assimilationist response of "bourgeoisie-oriented elites."[27] It is here suggested that black fraternities have had greater influence over existential realities than has been previously realized.

Even Howard Odum's widely cited 1910 exposition of the difference in development and kind of black Americans acknowledged that fraternal associations were of major influence and must be considered on the same level of importance as the home, school, and church. Using the Mississippi of his time as the basis for extrapolation, Odum found total membership in

24. Marvin E. Olsen, "Social and Political Participation of Blacks," *American Sociological Review*, pp. 682–97.

25. Myrdal, *An American Dilemma;* E. Franklin Frazier, *Black Bourgeoisie.*

26. Frederick Douglass, "What Are the Colored People Doing for Themselves," *Negro Social and Political Thought,* ed. Howard Brotz, pp. 203–8.

27. William A. Muraskin, *Middle Class Blacks in a White Society: Prince Hall Freemasonry in America,* p. 7.

fraternal societies approximately equal to church membership in most areas, but exceeding church membership in others.[28]

W. E. B. Du Bois, a pioneer in survey research, examined the black community in Philadelphia at the turn of the century. Du Bois noted the considerable attraction and importance that secret societies had upon members of the black community. He found the Odd Fellows, approximately 200,000 in number, to be the most important group in that period. He interpreted the attractiveness of the Odd Fellows, Freemasons, and others as "partly social intercourse" and "partly insurance," furnishing "pastime from the monotony of work, a field for ambition and intrigue, a chance for parade, and insurance against misfortune." He placed these institutions next in importance to the church and saw hope for the uplift of blacks by "mastery of the art of social organized life."[29] Du Bois and others to follow[30] have noted the opportunity provided by black organizations to acquire the satisfaction of achievement despite the wounding comparisons with the achievements of whites. Upward mobility and middle-class status was circumscribed for blacks by conditions existing under segregation.[31] Their positions were more precarious and less consistently recognized by others than for their counterparts. Charles Wesley talks of the black middle class:

> Generally, there was exclusion and non-participation in many professional, technical and social relations. The obstacles to professional and personal associations helped to make it difficult for a larger number of professionals to reach their goals of service through their desired standard of living. It was their task to advance the tone of the community socially, to educate the community and to elevate its economic interests . . .[32]

Black businesses have been important to the black community for this reason. Very few jobs were provided by these for they were usually small in number and scope and most often family-operated; but the businessman was still living proof that some measure of success could be attained. The importance of the

28. Howard W. Odum, *Social and Mental Traits of the Negro.*
29. W. E. B. Du Bois, *The Philadelphia Negro: A Social Study,* pp. 224–33.
30. See, for example, John Dollard, *Caste and Class in a Southern Town.*
31. Boulware, *The Oratory of Negro Leaders,* p. 41.
32. Charles H. Wesley, *Neglected History: Essays in Negro American History by a College President,* p. 24.

businessman and professional for the morale of the entire community cannot be overstated.

Much has been written about the gap between the middle and lower socioeconomic segments within the black community. Max Weber, during his 1904 visit to America, remarked upon the gap between the uneducated black rural masses and those he saw as the leaders of the race.[33] In addition to the rural-urban division was that in their line of their work many blacks had to exclude other blacks because their business, skill, or profit margin was geared to whites. Similarly situated blacks understood the reality of this situation. While the gap in dollar power has been and is real, there has been a stronger dimension of common purpose and identity due to consensus of the external threats to long-term black viability.[34] To expect blacks not to have class differences and not to form class-bound structures is unrealistic given the nature of democratic capitalism. A frictionless social universe is impossible since society is a patchwork of crisscrossing conflicts of component parts.[35] To expect the middle-class segment of any population to identify completely and beatifically with the lower class of that population is a sociological error. Pragmatism, however, has characterized the black experience of adjustment in the United States. If any generalization can be made, it would be that all blacks have been and are dissatisfied with the status accorded the race. The goal of all, from whatever ideological or activistic persuasion, is for the group and each individual to be labeled as socially, economically, and politically equal to all others, to earn status on the basis of one's own worth. The goal is still to be obtained.

The black achiever has sought support and gain in social

33. Ernst Manasee presents an insightful but too often neglected treatment of Weber's thoughts concerning America and race in general in "Max Weber on Race," *Social Research,* pp. 191–221.

34. Some consider a new divisive factor to be the growth and expansion of the black middle class servicing the public sector (one-third or more government resources) with a large black lower-class constituency. However, the impact of this should not be overexaggerated since a comparison can be made to the days of segregation when the middle class was composed of the principals, teachers, beauticians, and so forth, whose total clientele was the black population of all income levels.

35. Georg Simmel, *On Individuality and Social Forms,* ed. Donald N. Levine.

interactions. E. Franklin Frazier has done the most extensive work on stratification patterns within the black community. Focusing upon the "various forms of distinction" within the community, Frazier has argued that prior to the 1930s there were only two classes of American blacks: one stemming from the field experiences of slavery and the other, the middle class, stemming from the free blacks and household slaves. In the early decades of the twentieth century, he argued, the black "peasants" increasingly migrated and urbanized. Chances for economic advancement were available but often marred by the caste nature of the larger society. Frazier claimed that this situation produced a new middle class that he dubbed the black bourgeoisie. This strata no longer reflected the acculturated genteel tradition acquired by domestic service and missionary education. Frazier chose to view this as a negative development. While his interpretation can be faulted given more sophisticated methods of analysis, there are many insights:

> The relatively segregated life which the Negro lives makes him struggle to realize the values which give status within his group. An automobile, a home, a position as a teacher, or membership in a fraternity may confer a distinction in removing the possessor from an inferior social status that could never be appreciated by one who is a stranger to Negro life.[36]

The associational groupings of black achievers serve as buffers from the dissonance created between achieved status and ascribed status. Pragmatically, what better way was there to facilitate growth than by modeling the established organizational forms. A minority organization paralleling an acceptable and prestigious majority organization would be more likely to be accepted in the society than an unfamiliar form. It was advantageous for blacks and other minorities to attempt to associate themselves with the European tradition of secret societies. Unfamiliar forms of black organizations might arouse fears and reactionary responses, leading to another cause for the group's

36. E. Franklin Frazier, "La Bourgeoisie Noire," in *The Black Sociologists: The First Half-Century,* eds. John H. Bracey, Jr., August Meier, Elliott Rudwick. Frazier's article was originally written in 1929. See also Woodson, *The Negro Professional Man,* for an analysis of a comprehensive survey of blacks nationwide in the early 1930s. Woodson found that 75% of all black physicians were in fraternal orders; 71% of these officers of their organization. Half of the lawyers had multiple fraternal affiliations.

suppression or ineffectiveness.[37] It is suggested here that fraternal affiliations are best evaluated as realistic and pragmatic institutions providing encouragement for both the cultural aspirations of blacks and the quest for greater autonomy. Freemasonry may fill for blacks what Kurt Lewin has dubbed the social reality function of a group.[38] What is socially accepted as reality by the group is shaped and internalized by the group member. Parameters are established for interaction, impersonally proscribed and prescribed, offering assurance of order and security.

It is unfortunate that social scientists have too often ignored the pragmatic nature of minority adaptation patterns. Protective coloration is one rational, defensive adjustment process that has occurred and that can be seen manifested by the black experience in the United States. Affiliation with an organization duplicate in form and substance to that existent in mainstream society allowed the possibility that individuals could blunt the worse aspects of the handicap of minority stigmatization by emphasizing their achieved over their ascribed status.

37. Prince Hall Freemasonry is not syncretic in the sense of a mixture of African and European culture—that is, with the exception of the initial belief structure of every Mason that the roots of the brotherhood can be traced back to ancient Egyptian civilization. There is no evidence that American blacks ever attempted to emulate African secret societies. Melville Herskovits (*The American Negro*) is the foremost investigator of African continuities in the American experience. E. Franklin Frazier devoted much research to the refutation of the argument of continuities; he stressed that the American way of life stemmed from the experiences of slavery and from responses to the American environment. For a more recent discussion of this matter see Orlando Patterson, "Toward a Future That Has No Past—Reflections on the Fate of Blacks in the Americas," *The Public Interest*, where he concludes, after reviewing past studies, that while Africanisms such as folklore, rythmic patterning, and tonal intonations exist, there have been no African social institutions per se in the American black past.

38. See Kurt Lewin, *Resolving Social Conflicts: Selected Papers on Group Dynamics*.

Chapter 9

The Commitment of
Black Masons

"To be a Freemason in the latter part of the 18th century was accounted a rare distinction," for the order was "universally patronized by men of high degree," chronicles one historian of Masonry.[1] The white Masons in the colonies prior to the War of Independence symbolized strength of purpose and a promise of a better society to the freedmen. They were the power people, not the aristocrats stuck in false conservatism. As we examine the history of black Freemasonry we find that the most visible blacks, or those familiar by name to white society, were often Prince Hall Freemasons. Within the black community and, more recently, the larger community, they were the power people, the achievers seeking change. Throughout the entire history of Prince Hall Freemasonry, there have been numerous "black pioneers," the first in various positions and institutions.

Black Masons have been invisible to white society, and their existence and activities have not been acknowledged by society. Only white Masons, and perhaps not many of them, have remained aware of black Freemasonry. It is not total invisibility, however, for mention of black Masonic journals and affairs appear in white Masonic records from the beginning of the nineteenth century.[2] Masonic matters were evidently discussed in the colonies with blacks present: "It was customary for members of the Fraternity to speak of Masonic matters by indirection. For instance, if an . . . eavesdropper approached while Brethren were talking Masonry one would say, 'It rains.' This was the cue to turn the conversation."[3]

1. George W. Crawford, *Prince Hall and His Followers: Being a Monograph on the Legitimacy of Negro Masonry,* p. 111.
2. See Harold Van Buren Voorhis, *Negro Masonry in the United States,* preface. In addition, actions were taken by white bodies regarding these groups as has been discussed.
3. Melvin M. Johnson, *The Beginnings of Freemasonry in America,* pp. 52–53.

89

It could also be that paternalistic social attitudes blocked an awareness that blacks could function on the level of abstract philosophy. Blacks, being of a different kind, would not be attracted to and unable to comprehend the mysteries of Masonry. Thus there was no need to hide Masonic rituals from blacks. Robert Ezra Park, in the foremost sociological journal of 1918, wrote concerning the "distinctive racial temperament" and characteristics of blacks:

> These characteristics manifest themselves in a genial, sunny, and social disposition, in an interest and attachment to external, physical things rather than to subjective states and objects of introspection; in a disposition for expression rather than enterprise and action ... the Negro because of his natural attachment to known familiar objects, places and persons, is pre-adapted to conservatism and to local and personal loyalties ... under very discouraging circumstances. I once heard Kelly Miller, the most philosophical of the leaders and teachers of his race, say in a public speech that one of the greatest hardships the Negro suffered in this country was due to the fact that he was not permitted to be patriotic.[4]

The persistence of this paternalistic disdain lends support for the casual treatment or neglect of black Masons by their white brethren in Freemasonry.[5]

From the minority perspective, secret society membership in the late eighteenth and nineteenth centuries was one way of adjusting to the realities of minority status. By presenting oneself to peers and to superordinate others in an appropriately prestigious role and setting, one could hope for a change in the other's definition, particularly since the very act of joining or duplicating in practice an esteemed mainstream organization provided valuable information of intent.[6]

Freemasonry also offered shelter in an unstable environment.[7] Masonic membership was particularly important for those individuals whose business affairs required travel, for it

4. Robert Ezra Park, *Race and Culture.*

5. In a pioneering study of secret societies, Noel Gist noted that one of the characteristics of secret societies has been racial purity. See "Secret Societies: A Cultural Study of Fraternalism in the United States," *The University of Missouri Studies.*

6. See Edward N. Palmer, "Negro Secret Societies," *Social Forces,* pp. 207–12.

7. This occurred for each minority group individual who turned to affiliation in a secret society. See, for example, Stanford M. Lyman, "Chinese

entitled the traveler to welcome and sustenance in unfamiliar surroundings. In the days of segregation, this aspect has been most important for American blacks; it has been of similar importance to Jewish and other minority Masons. Masonic membership could on occasion mean the difference between life and death. Each individual Mason, upon initiation, swears that he will aid a fellow Mason in distress. A secret sign is taught to the new members, a distress signal conveyed by placing hands to forehead, palms frontward, thumbs and index fingers forming an equilateral triangle. The middle line of the head and upper and lower arms complete the triangle.

Stories abound of the utility of such signals. Army Colonel McKisty (or McKinstry), a white Mason, is said to have been saved from burning at the stake at the hands of the Indian allies of the British during the Revolutionary War when Mohawk Chief Joseph Brant, initiated into Masonry by the British, intervened on his behalf. The officer was given safe conduct to Quebec.[8]

An Indian Mason is said to have recognized the Masonic sign of distress as early as 1660. Rev. Morgan Jones, a chaplain on a military expedition from Port Royal, South Carolina, was taken prisoner by the Tuscarora Indians. The Sachem of the Doeg tribe recognized the Masonic signal and interceded, freeing the chaplain from danger.[9] Another incident is recorded in the nineteeth century. A Scotsman, McGrath, came to the colonies in 1765 with his family. He had tattoed the Masonic square and compass with the letter *G* on the son's left breast. This son married a Seneca Indian and went to live with the tribe. When his granddaughter became lost, he set out to find her. Captured by the Cherokees, he was about to be killed when the tattoo became visible as his body was stripped. Since the chief of the tribe was a Mason, McGrath was spared and adopted into the Cherokee tribe.[10] During the Civil War, northern prisoners who were Masons are said to have been released or smuggled from southern prisons by their Masonic brothers. Stories also

Secret Societies in the Occident: Some Notes and Suggestions for Research in the Sociology of Secrecy," *Canadian Review of Sociology and Anthropology*.

8. Ray V. Denslow, *The Masonic World of Ray Denslow*, ed. Lewis C. Cook.

9. Ibid., p. 42.

10. Ibid., p. 39.

are told of the general value of Masonic ties during the Gold Rush and the westward movement of the nation.

This is not to say that all distress signals were recognized. Mormon leader Joseph Smith gave the Masonic signal of distress just before he was murdered and even uttered, "Oh Lord, my God, is there no help for the Widow's Son?" Both pleas were ignored as he was shot by muskets.[11] However, it is also alleged that his earlier escape from jail in Missouri was arranged by friendly Masons.

Masonic membership has been of particular importance for blacks. During interviews with black Masons, some recalled events of Masonic assistance in tense situations. One gentleman described a situation during the Depression when he owed a substantial amount of property taxes. He, and two others in a similar spot, were arrested by the constable for nonpayment of the debt. Seeing the Masonic ring, the judge abated the debt.[12]

More important than the protection offered by Masonic responsibilities, if and when executed, has been the sense of mission offered by the philosophy. It appears that black Masons, like other minority Masons, have consistently felt that a sense of personal worth could be enhanced by labeling oneself and one's enlightened peers as catalysts for a better world. It seems likely that verification of the success deemed important by the larger society might seem attainable by a circuitous route: Masonic brotherhood. Minorities sought the additional safety and protection accruing from Masonic affiliation and hoped that the aura of respectability and power might prove transmutable.[13]

Examining the journals and records of Prince Hall Freemasonry indicates the predominance of physicians, lawyers, clergymen, businessmen, and educators. One also notes the familiarity of the names. Black Masons have not only been in leadership positions in the community but have also been at the forefront of race-related efforts.

The unusually high proportion of clergymen is intriguing

11. Jerald Tanner and Sandra Tanner, *Mormonism: Shadow or Reality?*, p. 485; J. H. Adamson, "The Treasure of the Widow's Son."

12. Interview, April 1974.

13. Roy Canning has suggested the same of Mormon Masons. Canning has also hypothesized that Masonic affiliation may have been of particular import for Joseph Smith. Although most of his lieutenants were of similar persuasion, Smith might have been able to assure better control of dissenters through their double hierarchical ties with Freemasonry.

considering the initial resistance to Freemasonry on the part of some clergy, white and black. Methodist clergymen were particularly well represented in the early years: Prince Hall, Richard Allen, and Absolum Jones are readily recognizable persons. Another prominent churchman and Freemason was Rev. Theodore S. Wright, an early Princeton graduate, who was active in the antislavery movement. Wright served on the board of managers and the executive committee of the American Anti-Slavery Society in the 1830s. A persuasive orator, he spoke throughout the East concerning the pitfalls of various colonization schemes being suggested under the rubric of abolitionism.[14]

Clergy, from parish levels to bishops, have been and are still prominently represented in Prince Hall Freemasonry. One intriguing Masonic figure of the mid-twentieth century listed in the 1944 *Who's Who in Colored America* was Arnold Josiah Ford, a black rabbi from the West Indies. A music teacher and bandmaster, Rabbi Ford composed the Ethiopian National Anthem before founding Congregation Beth B'nai Abraham in 1924, a synagogue for "Aethiopian (Orthodox) Jews" in America. His congregation was composed of believers in Judaism from the West Indies, "Arabia," Abyssinia, and eastern countries.[15]

Support for Marvin Olsen's ethnic-community thesis that persons who strongly identify with their ethnicity have greater involvement, is demonstrated by the abundance of prime movers for black advancement. Such an activist was James Forten of Philadelphia, an abolitionist and leader in the Negro Convention Movement of the 1830s. Booker T. Washington, a formidable person of influence in his time, found it expedient to be a Mason. Washington, designated by whites as the leading spokesperson for blacks in the early twentieth century, had enormous influence upon patterns of relations between blacks and whites. His connection with the men and institutions of political power assured him access to a group of people whom he assumed would take the lead in establishing a just system of

---

14. See Harry E. Davis, *A History of Freemasonry Among Negroes in America*, pp. 176–77; August Meier and Elliott Rudwick, *From Plantation to Ghetto*, chapter three.

15. For more information, see Thomas Yenser, ed., *Who's Who in Colored America*.

societal operation. The leading officers of the black lodges, particularly in the South, supported Washington's Tuskeegee operation.[16]

Over the years, other prominent individuals have been active in Prince Hall Freemasonry. A tally of contemporary public figures would include the following: Tom Bradley, former mayor of Los Angeles; Mayor Maynard Jackson of Atlanta; Andrew Young, former ambassador to the United Nations; the late president of Liberia, William Tubman; Supreme Court Justice Thurgood Marshall; civil rights leader Rev. Benjamin Hooks of the National Association for the Advancement of Colored People; businessman John Johnson of the Ebony Publishing Corporation; the late Daniel "Chappie" James, military officer; musicians Count Basie, the late Duke Ellington, and Lionel Hampton. But an examination of lesser known figures of the past presents a clearer view of the typical Prince Hall Mason and presents even more forceful support for the contention that Freemasons are involved as individuals and as a collective in the improvement of the local community, city, state, and world.

Freemasonry has been a proud organization unwilling to remain a secret society in the black community. Masons repeatedly stress that it is a society with certain secrets rather than a secret society. These persons proudly declare their Masonic affiliation and share readily the long litany of predecessors in the benevolent society and their achievements. A look at the records from a northern urban center—Cincinnati—in the latter part of the nineteenth and early twentieth centuries illustrates the types of individuals within the ranks of black Freemasonry. George W. Conrad, one of the original Ohio Prince Hall Masons before the Civil War, was a contractor and builder who served in the Civil War.[17] Joe Early, a chef and pastrymaker, was lauded by such political figures as Grant, Hayes, and Garfield when he was a cook for an army colonel. In addition to his culinary abilities, Early was a mail carrier.[18] Charles A. Schooley, a black dentist with a white clientele, was prominent in both Freemasonry and the Republican party, as was George W. Hays, who at fourteen had been forced to serve in the Confederate

16. Robert L. Factor, *The Black Response to America.*
17. Wendell P. Dabney, *Cincinnati's Colored Citizens.*
18. Ibid., p. 80.

Army but escaped to join the Union forces. Hays waited tables while attending school, eventually worked on surveying teams, and later became an assemblyman. While active in the Freemasons, he was also an Odd Fellow and a True Reformer.[19] Along with these men were lawyers, politicians, military officers, barbers, Pullman porters, grocery store owners, real estate agents, contract haulers, clergymen, tailors, and an abundance of post office workers: middle-class achievers within the black class structure. Again, one is struck by the fact that Freemasonry has continued to appeal to this segment of the black middle class despite the lack of white Masonic recognition. As one author wrote: "In spite of its ideal of a world-wide brotherhood, Masonry has often failed, when put to the test, to transcend the limitations of nationalism and sometimes even of racial and religious differences within a nation."[20]

A few black individuals have been initiated into Freemasonry by local white subordinate lodges, but it appears that they were expected to form black lodges rather than attempt to maintain active permanent membership in the white lodge. The first is said to have been Paul Drayton of Charleston, South Carolina, in the early nineteenth century. Drayton later organized a black lodge, which leads one to suspect that the process of acceptance differed for Drayton than for his white fellow initiates. It could also be that initiation into the first degree did not necessarily indicate permanent membership in a particular subordinate lodge.[21]

It is interesting that this occurred first in the South and that there was a relative degree of latent support among a minority of white Masons toward the separate function of black Masonic organizations. Some informants suggest a logical explanation: the reality of genuine kinship ties. Many white Masons knew that some of their blood relations were black Masons, which perhaps accounts for the willingness to ease things for relatives who could not otherwise be recognized. In Kentucky, for exam-

19. Ibid., pp. 231, 248. Multiple memberships are a common pattern within Freemasonry, the Odd Fellows, the Elks, and fraternities.
20. Frank H. Hankins, "Masonry," *Encyclopedia of the Social Sciences,* p. 183.
21. Harry E. Davis, "Documents Relating to Negro Masonry in America," *Journal of Negro History,* chapter fourteen.

ple, the grandfather of a black initiated in 1925 was helped by his white half-brother to set up a black lodge.[22]

In other instances, light-skinned blacks are known to have been members of white lodges. In the 1870s and 1880s, for example, there were two blacks known to be members of a white lodge in Cleveland. Dr. Leonidas Wilson was a dentist who was fair-complexioned but readily identifiable as black. While he did not deny his heritage, his clientele and associates were white. John H. Hope, similarly light-skinned, served a term as master of the lodge. Initially there was tension:

> It appears that after his election to that office some question was raised. Hope had never denied his lineage nor attempted to sail under false colors. He offered to resign his office and to demit to one of the Prince Hall Lodges in Cleveland, but his own lodge, with full knowledge of all the circumstances, declined his offer and he remained in the lodge.[23]

In this same period, a black Boston caterer and state legislator was also a functioning member of a local white lodge.

There have also been a few occasions, so it is said, when white Masons have rendered Masonic burial rites for a black. The case of Bert Williams, an early black entertainer, is an example. Williams, who had broken with the American minstrel tradition in the early 1900s, was viewed as a radical in his initiation of black musical theater. Although minstrelsy was originated by slaves as satirical derision of the white plantation class, it was taken over and transformed by white showmen. Ironically, what started out as ridicule of whites was eventually used by whites for ridicule of blacks. Adding insult to injury, by the 1860s the only way a black actor could play the minstrel shows was by smearing his face with burnt cork and painting his lips a hideous white, ending up as a caricature of black people. Williams refused to bow to this; he ended up with the Ziegfield Follies for over a decade.[24]

A Pennsylvania black lodge has interesting roots in an all-white lodge in an aristocratic suburb of Pittsburgh. In 1890,

22. George W. Crawford, *The Prince Hall Counsellor: A Manual of Guidance Designed to Aid Those Combatting Clandestine Freemasonry*, p. 57.

23. Davis, *History of Freemasonry*, p. 179.

24. See Charles H. Wesley, *The History of the Prince Hall Grand Lodge of Free and Accepted Masons of the State of Ohio, 1849–1917*, for mention of this event.

when an eminent old-school jurist was grand master, four blacks applied for membership. Judge J. W. White of the Common Plea Court of Allegheny County held to the letter of the Masonic law. He insisted that the usual investigation be conducted by an unbiased committee, and as a result the four men were admitted in the usual manner. The Grand Lodge of Pennsylvania was incensed by this action, but issued what it considered a reasonable request because of the eminence of the lodge and its officials. Grand Master White was to apologize for his actions and promise not to again offend the sensibilities of the white members by admitting blacks. Judge White refused and vigorously reiterated his intention to do the same if the occasion arose. The Grand Lodge of Pennsylvania then suspended St. John's Lodge No. 50 for ninety-nine years. Thus, the lodge and its elaborate lodge hall could not legally operate. The white body chose to act in a manner befitting their stance:

> . . . on June 24, 1891 in a hall opposite to the St. John's lodge rooms, twenty-six colored men were initiated into Masonry by authority of the (Prince Hall) Grand Lodge of Pennsylvania. On the night when its officers were installed, the entire equipment of St. John's lodge was turned over to the colored brethren and they were warranted under the name and number of the suspended lodge—St. John's No. 50. One can see a certain poetic Masonic justice in this incident.[25]

Temporary situations of joint effort have occurred, sometimes by chance. For example, an 1843 cornerstone-laying ceremony in St. Louis was an integrated affair of black and white Masons although this was not the intention of the white body. It became known during the occasion that some of the members of the black minstrel band on hand for the event were Masons.[26]

Some evidence exists that visitations by white Masons to black lodges did occur, particularly during the nineteenth century. More frequently, white lodges have allowed black Masons to use their libraries as long as they continued to function as a separate body instead of requesting kinship affiliation or obligations. The legitimation of social intermingling between black

---

25. Davis, *History of Freemasonry,* pp. 173–74.

26. As is commonly known, Masons have traditionally officiated at the cornerstone laying of government and public buildings. This particular incident is described in Denslow, *The Masonic World of Ray Denslow,* ed. Lewis C. Cook, p. 146.

and white Masons has remained anathema in mainstream Freemasonry.[27]

A monograph circulated among black Masons in the early twentieth century spoke specifically to the question of how black Masons could and should treat white Masons. George Crawford spoke of the "difficulty of deciding how to treat those regular Masons in the manner which their own unMasonic attitude deserves, and yet be consistent and true to Masonic vows." Alternative strategies were discussed. Returning like treatment was discarded as a nonviable and counterproductive alternative; although blacks were the victims, inferiority would still be assumed by the public. The best alternative, it was suggested, was to "be aloof; except to those individuals who treat black Masons as equals." They were exhorted to hold their heads high as did Prince Hall, the founding father. Why desire to join with "petty men"? "The only recognition which Negro Masons could ever accept without self-stultification would be recognition coupled with union with them under the wide baldachin (canopy) of universal Masonry, from which the white brethren have drawn themselves apart. As to recognition on any other basis—a fig!"[28]

An article geared to a white Masonic audience around the time of World War I by Prince Hall Grand Historian Arthur Schomburg states:

> What the Prince Hall Masons are seeking is only non-inter-ference with their humble patrimony . . . Prince Hall Masons in America are the last persons who are desirous of promiscuously slipping into white lodges to be purposively denied a privilege well known as an inherent right of the subordinate lodge. He may look for that expression of brotherhood abroad where, in the language of Burns, "a man is a man for a' that anda' that" and where men are schooled in the true elements that go to make the universality of the craft and where Masonry is the real handmaid of the Christian religion.[29]

27. Nicholas Babchuk and Ralph V. Thompson, "The Voluntary Association of Negroes," *American Sociological Review;* William Muraskin, *Middle Class Blacks in a White Society.*

28. Crawford, *Prince Hall and His Followers,* p. 89.

29. Arthur A. Schomburg, "Freemasonry Versus 'An Inferior Race: Rejoinder Made to Recent Articles by One Who Speaks for Negro Masonry."

The belief that European Freemasonry adheres to the true principles of the brotherhood has sustained the black Mason. Various Prince Hall Masonic documents cite European lodges as nondiscriminatory and describe American white Masonry as a deviation: "It is no longer the true and plain Masonry handed down to us, but as provided by a variety of American people who have injected all their prejudices and their 'beautiful abstractions' by which evasion can be kept up."[30] One finds news items in Prince Hall Masonic materials concerning hospitality and awards given to black Masons by European lodges. A photo in a 1906 issue of *Alexander's Magazine,* for example, shows a medal being presented to Most Worshipful Brother Fredric Monroe upon his election to office in the Massachusetts grand lodge, Prince Hall, by his Hamburg, Germany, counterpart. The German Mason is quoted as saying that "we are all children of the same Father in Heaven."[31]

But the European Masons were by no means nondiscriminatory. In the early twentieth century, English Masons excluded German, Austrian, Hungarian, and Turkish people from their lodges. The black perception of their adherence to Masonic ideals is understandable, however, given the public posture of European Masons toward black American Freemasonry. Masonic recognition was extended by bodies such as the Grand Orient of France. In other instances, European bodies formally protested the prejudicial operation of mainstream American lodges.[32] From a distance, lip service was easily given and integrity assumed.

Prince Hall Masons over the years have chosen to identify with universal Masonry as they perceive it and its normative potential rather than dwell upon the ill-treatment received from the American mainstream body. They have, however, remained constantly aware of the dilemma. W. G. Runciman's distinction between normative and comparative reference groups is useful in explaining the loyalty of blacks. While both terms apply to social models, Runciman suggests that normative groups—those supplying approved standards—exercise a more powerful

30. Ibid.
31. Walter J. Stevens, "Masonic Literature," *Alexander's Magazine,* pp. 22–24.
32. Davis, *A History of Freemasonry,* p. 111.

influence for identification purposes than the comparative groups.[33] A leading black Mason has stated:

> Recognition is, of course, a desirable privilege. It promotes fraternal growth, preserves fraternal contact, aids in the transfer of membership, and enables the interchange of thought and ideas between those having a common purpose. But the failure to recognize is not a decree of outlawry as some seem to think; it does not affect the standing of either body or its constituent membership; and it is not a judicial determination of any issue of law or fact. It simply means that one body does not desire fellowship with another, just as one individual may not desire the acquaintance and companionship of another.[34]

"The Prince Hall Mason . . . is unalterably opposed to even a suggestion of amalgamation between the two fraternities," stated Harry A. Williamson, Prince Hall historian, in 1924.[35] The black Masons pride themselves on their true adherence to Masonic ideals in contrast to the action of the "colorphobists":

> Despite imposed disabilities some advantages are held by the Prince Hall Masons because of certain traits characteristic of Negro people. These people have a firm belief in the efficiency of prayer. It matters not what the nature of the project, it is invariably sanctified by them with preliminary prayer. In the Masonic lodge the black man offers his invocation to the same Divine Arbiter as does his white brother; but the intention, fervency and faith of the former has a higher degree of intensity. He pleads that the spirit of love may descend upon all men and Masons regardless of color or location.[36]

This sentiment of faithful adherence to implicit religious principles serves as a support system for the black Mason, who tends to be flexible in the face of paradox. The editor of one of the black Masonic periodicals, *Masonic Quarterly Review,* talked about the white fear of social intercourse: "We believe men, no matter of what race, can respect each other without the hobby of raising the dust of social equality. What we demand and are entitled to is plain justice, nothing but equality before the law."[37]

33. W. G. Runciman, *Relative Deprivation and Social Justice.*
34. Davis, *History of Freemasonry,* p. 111.
35. Williamson, "Legitimacy of Negro Masonry," *National Fraternal Review,* p. 4.
36. Harry A. Williamson, "The Position of Negro Masonry," *National Trestle Board.*
37. Schomburg, "An Inferior Race," p. 27.

Pragmatically, some argue that the matter should be resolved for a coalition of efforts:

> First where the concerted effort of all regular Masonic bodies regardless of color or race is desired for particular reasons, a direct appeal to those regular bodies would without a doubt obtain the desired goal; second, the fight against bogus Masonry would be greatly enhanced by such recognition; third, the confusion that now exists as to the determination as to who is regular and who is not would be eliminated.[38]

On an individual basis, however, the clear majority of Prince Hall Masons surveyed in this study want only "their rightful place in the sun," which would stem from Masonic recognition. A minority theme had been repeatedly articulated: "The stigma of bastardy," argues Crawford, is of concern to black Masons "not so much because it might bar his reception into polite society, but to vindicate himself in the eyes of his own self respect."[39] This need for white validation does not appear to be a widespread motivating concern. One can measure the importance of Prince Hall autonomy through the voices of past and present black Masons and through examination of the fraternal literature. For example, sampling the Buffalo, New York, journal, *The Pyramid,* for the past thirty years, shows that while general discrimination was mentioned in small items in 1946, 1956, and 1966, there was not a single entry concerning racism nor the need to integrate. The absence can be interpreted as lack of concern, acceptance of reality, or as an indication of the pragmatic aspects of the situation.

In 1965, a white Mason and historian of Freemasonry, championing the cause of Prince Hall Freemasonry, wrote:

> One of the paradoxical elements in this problem is that over a long period of time Prince Hall Masonry has developed its own bureaucratic hierarchy, paralleling those of the Caucasian grand lodges, and those Past and Present Grand Lodge officers are jealous of their position and prestige in their own circles, therefore practically all of them want "recognition," NOT any "Union," for that would mean that even if they were given "Past" grand rank, that thereafter they would expect at best

38. Vidal A. MacKinnon, *Proceedings of the Most Worshipful Prince Hall Grand Lodge.* Free and Accepted Masons of Massachusetts, pp. 25–26.
39. Crawford, *The Prince Hall Counsellor,* p. 110.

only District Deputy Grand Masters, with the chance of an occasional Grand Master.[40]

That so much effort by black and white Freemasonry has been necessarily devoted to the issue of social intercourse is unfortunate. As Kelly Miller stated in 1910:

> The charge that the educated Negro is in quest of social affiliation with the whites is absurdly untrue. His sense of self-respect effectively forbids forcing himself upon any unwelcome association. The Negro is building up his own society based upon character, culture, and the nice amenities of life, and can find ample social satisfaction within the limits of his own race.[41]

The issue of Masonic recognition, or lack of it, points to the overlap of the societal climate of discrimination upon the fraternal body of Masonry. Editorials in contemporary Masonic bulletins charge that institutionalized racism in the white Masonic order continues to maintain the appalling paradox of segregation within a brotherhood.

40. Harvey N. Brown. *Freemasonry Among Negroes and Whites in America,* p. 35.

41. Kelly Miller, *Race Adjustment: Essays on the Negro in America.*

Chapter 10

The Middle-Class Phenomenon

The persistence of isomorphism in the diversity of stratification patterns of the black community is a social fact, historically
and sociologically.[1] This has influenced, and will continue to
influence, both the black community and the future social realities of this country. Pillarization by race, despite class and
interest similarity, suggests that future problems in the United
States cannot be reduced to class, as suggested by neo-Marxists.
Pillarization, however, does not necessarily imply divisiveness
for the future; in fact, it may be a meaningful mechanism for
racial and ethnic harmony.[2]

The question arises as to why there has been so little work
done in this area of parallel organizations and institutions in
terms of either descriptive or theoretical analysis. One explanation is that undue attention has been focused on cyclical theories
of minority responses and, more recently, on integration versus
separatism, an unnecessary zero-sum dichotomy. Further,
American blacks have often been discussed in terms of traits and
characteristics labeled as the "mark of oppression."[3] The persistence of this concept is remarkable given that, among its other
deficits, the data base for this "pioneering" study was a mere
twenty-five psychoanalytic case studies. A composite of black

1. Donald Warren's comprehensive study of black communities offers
further support beyond this study. He concludes that racially distinct social
institutions appear to be an enduring phenomenon. See Donald I. Warren,
Black Neighborhoods: An Assessment of Community Power.
2. For an opposing argument see Orlando Patterson, *Ethnic Chauvinism:
The Reactionary Impulse.*
3. Abram Kardiner and L. Ovesey, *The Mark of Oppression.* Their study
dealt with the attempts of twenty-five black psychiatric clients to deal with
the low esteem accorded them by the wider society (author's interpretation). The attempt to act white when frustrated at the inability to attain
higher status was said to stem from self-contempt triggered by low self-
esteem. Whites were said to be idealized, positive reference groups; blacks,
negatively valued and shunned.

maladaptation to the castelike nature of the American black experience has been extrapolated from this, a dangerous extrapolation of a biased stereotype. It fails to take into consideration the structural, environmental, and situational factors. More importantly, it deflects attention from the basic and continuing preponderance of well-adjusted minority individuals.

A valid study of a black middle class must examine the social science literature on marginality and status inconsistency. Everett Hughes has spoken of the educated black as having a status dilemma to resolve. He contends that such a person is a living contradiction since he or she is a "member of a group assigned a very humble and limited status" that at the same time bears "other characteristics which ordinarily give or allow the individual to acquire higher status."[4] Social science literature dealing with social class is voluminous, contradictory in particular areas, but in agreement that individuals have multiple rankings.[5] The subjects of our initial interest, the free black craftsmen of the eighteenth century, were high on occupational status but low on color ranking. According to theoretical formulations, status inconsistency occurs when the correlation between one's rankings on various status dimensions is low.

Early formulations posited a move by such status-inconsistent individuals or groups toward "equilibration, or balance."[6] The individual or group would be the initiator of action to restore a sense of balance. Emile Benoit-Smullyan saw this as the motivating factor behind revolutionary social change or upheaval.[7] Gerhard Lenski, however, allows for a variety of responses. His study, often cited and presently the most comprehensive work in this area, discusses the nature of class systems and conceptualizes the inconsistency in demands placed upon an individual or group due to different levels of placement in various social subsystems: politics, property, occupation, ethnicity, and so

4. See Everett C. Hughes's discussion of the marginal man as cultural hybrid in "Social Change and Status Protest: An Essay on the Marginal Man," *Phylon*, pp. 58–65.

5. Emile Benoit-Smullyan, "Status, Status Types and Status Interrelations," *American Sociological Review*, pp. 151–61; Gerhard E. Lenski, "Status Crystallization: A Non-Vertical Dimension of Social Status," *American Sociological Review*, pp. 405–13; Lenski, *Power and Privilege*.

6. Benoit-Smullyan, "Status," *American Sociological Review*, pp. 151–61.

7. Lenski, *Power and Privilege*, and Crane C. Brinton, *The Anatomy of Revolution*, have further investigated this aspect.

forth. But the discipline of sociology cannot state that knowledge of an individual's various rankings can accurately predict the nature of his or her reaction. Few studies have empirically examined the specific combination of high achieved status combined with low ascribed status, with race or color as the latter variable. Most sociological studies of status avoid dealing with race not because of its unimportance but because of the magnitude of differences and difficulties accruing with the introduction of this variable. The literature that does consider race has focused upon dysfunctional adaptations.[8] Much of the literature on status inconsistency has focused upon pronounced stressful, nonfunctional reactions, inferring this to be the usual form of adaptation or, at least, the most frequent.

A basic assumption underlying this study is that members of the black middle class in the United States are subject to strains due to the discrepancies in status related to being achievers occupationally or socioeconomically while labeled as lower in status due to racial ascription. John Dollard raised the following hypothesis in 1937, which has yet to be adequately tested: "Strain on the individual personality undoubtedly differs as between the castes and classes. An hypothesis, which needs to be tested, is that it is greatest in the middle-class Negro group for the reason that severe impulse restriction is enjoined without appropriate compensation from the status side."[9] Certain institutional behavior among middle-class blacks has resulted in response to this status incongruity. It appears that while a subordinate group, racial or otherwise, may attempt to offset a negative definition of itself by accentuating unique cultural achievements, the greater the group's dependence upon the superordinate group for survival and success the more it will pattern itself after the latter in an attempt to reap rights, rewards, and privileges.

The black middle class has rarely been analyzed, and an institution such as Prince Hall Freemasonry provides insight because its membership includes men who are more in touch with the average black middle-class man than are the media-created spokespersons. Is marginality and status inconsistency a phenomenon for these men?

8. See, for example, E. F. Jackson, "Status Consistency and Symptoms of Stress," *American Sociological Review*, pp. 469–79.
9. John Dollard, *Caste and Class in a Southern Town*, p. 90.

The theoretical social science literature in this area is rooted in the work of Georg Simmel. Simmel, lecturing during the late nineteenth and early twentieth centuries, was a German Jew who experienced marginality himself due to anti-Semitism and his peripheral attachment to academia. Concerned with the positive and negative aspects of conflict, he was particularly interested in the multiple tensions inherent in the relationship between individual and society. Simmel believed that a person inevitably becomes involved in social relationships supporting or impeding his individuality. Conflict can strengthen dignity and self-esteem in these social interactions.[10] The task of sociology, maintained Simmel, is to study forms of human sociality according to the contents (the needs, drives, and purposes that lead individuals to associate with others) and forms (the synthesizing processes of human combination).[11]

Two major viewpoints can be distinguished in the ensuing literature: marginality as misfortune having negative psychological consequences and marginality as positive potential leading to creative ingenuity.[12] Simmel, Robert Ezra Park, Thorstein Veblen, and Melvin Seeman see the potential good in the greater objectivity of the marginal individual who has successfully adjusted, enabling him or her to challenge the givens of the social system. Seeman's major thesis is that marginal status provides the opportunity for the development of perspective and creativity in the realm of ideas. Milton Goldberg, however, speaks of marginality as offering a normative culture as an alternative. He states:

> The problem of the marginal culture, then, as long as its existence is conceived as necessary or desirable, would seem to be one of fulfilling its major goals of providing its members security, adequate facilities for participation in group life, and the opportunity to express their own cultural interests, without at

10. Harry Stack Sullivan, Carl Rogers, Abraham Maslow, and others have been particularly interested in the role of interaction in an individual's search for identity and worth. Cooley, Mead, and their successors have argued that the way one looks at himself or herself is a product of social experience.
11. Georg Simmel, *On Individuality and Social Forms*.
12. Melvin Seeman, "Intellectual Perspective and Adjustment to Minority Status," *Social Problems*, pp. 142–53.

the same time making them in appearance and behavior distinguishable from the members of the dominant culture.[13]

While Goldberg's use and meaning of the term *marginal culture* is ambiguous, it lends support to an interpretation that black Freemasonry serves as an insulator against the psychologically negative effects of marginality.

The body of literature on reference group theory[14] would also support the idea that an individual subject to conflicting pressures experiences various degrees of stress which he or she may choose to relieve by opting for one element to the exclusion of the other or by attempting to compromise in some form. Herbert Hyman is generally credited as the first to synthesize in formal fashion the various elements of what is now referred to as reference group theory. He found that individuals evaluated themselves positively or negatively in comparison with others designated as reference individuals, and that individuals primarily tended to choose comparisons that favor themselves. Generally, theoretical constructs concerning reference groups speak of comparative, aspirational, and normative groups.[15] The comparative reference group is that with which one compares oneself in terms of attributes and situations when making a judgment concerning self or membership group. The second, aspirational reference group, is that group from which an individual aspires to gain or maintain acceptance via participation since a reference group is not necessarily coterminous with a present membership group. Less attention within the body of reference group theory has been paid to predominantly normative reference groups. Analysis of the minority group experience with Freemasonry sheds some light in this area.

Relative deprivation theories, variants of reference group

---

13. Milton M. Goldberg, "A Qualification of the Marginal Man Theory," *American Sociological Review*, p. 58.

14. Herbert Hyman, "The Psychology of Status," *Archives of Psychology*, p. 269; Robert K. Merton and Alice Rossi, "Contributions to the Theory of Reference Group Behavior," *Social Theory and Social Structure*, ed. Robert K. Merton; Tamotsu Shibutani, "Reference Groups as Perspectives," *American Journal of Sociology*, pp. 562–69; Raymond Schmitt, *The Reference Other Orientation: An Extension of the Reference Group Concept.*

15. Tamotsu Shibutani, *Society and Personality: An Interactionist Approach to Social Psychology.*

theory, hold that individuals tend to compare their situational context with others in the same category (ascribed or achieved), defined according to the particular context, in forming an opinion of the existence of equitable justice or legitimacy.[16] Direct social contact with this comparative group is not necessary, but knowledge and perceived judgment of the group are required. An individual will choose a reference group that will foster and reinforce the positive identity he or she seeks to establish or maintain. Black identification patterns are a particular case of reference group behavior. Following Hyman, and refinements of his concept, one can observe that Freemasonry serves the function of comparative, aspirational, and normative reference group for black Masons. The prestige bestowed on Masons by association—whether real or imputed—in apparently close brotherhood with prominent and powerful people in the community and in the larger society is a particularly strong appeal of Freemasonry. Similarly, Robert Merton's status set theory deals with the variations of dominance, salience, and centrality of the multiple roles required by multiple categories.[17] Consistent with this concept, then, it can be seen that the salient status of Mason was being presented for recognition by wider society.

Prince Hall Masons appear to have hoped that Masonic ideology would have the power to motivate white Masons to reevaluate the black man's position in America. By adherence to the dictates of the ideology, the mainstream Masons would move to eradicate the racial contradictions in the new society. It is true, as Masonic historians claim, that many of the founding fathers of our nation were stalwart Masons. Thus, the black men of the eighteenth century who were attracted to Freemasonry perceived a possibility for neutralizing the conflicting strains within the society. The ideology was to be the integrative mechanism, facilitating change by producing and maintaining a basis for solidarity. The belief was utopian; whether or not it was

16. Merton, "Contributions to the Theory of Reference Group Behavior," *Social Theory and Social Structure,* ed. Robert K. Merton; Muzafer Sherif and Carolyn Sherif, *Reference Groups;* W. G. Runciman, *Relative Deprivation and Social Justice.*

17. A most useful exposition of this concept is presented in Cynthia F. Epstein, *Woman's Place.* Epstein's concern is with the multiple role requirements inherent in being female.

an illusion, Masonic affiliation was an attempt to create a more satisfying reality for black men of achievement.

Masonic involvement for minorities has absorbed and made bearable both the elements of risk in free-thinking ambition as well as society's negative lumping together of all blacks into the lumpenproletariat of ascribed status. Freemasonry must also be viewed as offering to its members an explanatory worldview. The gemeinschaft nature of Masonic lodges is complemented by the predictability inherent in a consistent and coherent worldview. The ideology of Freemasonry supplies a structured order in a member's life by offering as its most unique possession insight into, and commitment to, a systematic and comprehensive belief structure.

For a minority-group member, affiliation in a secret society clearly establishes one as a selected individual, sharing in secrets of great import. Any anxieties about marginal status, irrespective of substance, are removed from visiblity in the intensity of the association. Secrecy itself no longer exerts major drawing power for either mainstream or minority, although it is by no means immaterial.[18] But the maintenance of some closure on "inside" information is salient for the brotherhood as an integrative mechanism. The nonsecret aspects of Freemasonry appear to have more social significance: it is important to be known as a selected member or official of a select society, a highly ethical brotherhood having worldwide prestigious recognition.

It is intriguing, from the data perused, that no indication was found of any overflowing of hostility from the general citizenry toward the black Masonic organizations during the periods of the most intense anti-Masonic efforts in the United States. David Brian Davis's intensive treatment of the themes of the organized nineteenth-century anti-Masonic movement found no hint of specifics against black groups.[19] Thus, membership offered civic status, albeit limited.

18. Walton Hannah, in *Darkness Visible: A Revelation and Interpretation of Freemasonry*, p. 10, states that the only secret of Freemasonry is that there is not any such thing as a specific Masonic secret. Hannah, a disillusioned Mason, views the brotherhood as a gigantic bluff based on complacent assumptions.

19. See David Brian Davis, "Some Themes of Counter-Subversion: An Analysis of Anti-Masonic, Anti-Catholic, and Anti-Mormon Literature," for

On the individual level, a major motivating factor for organizational participation appears to be the opportunity for reinforcement of a positive self-image. The acquisition of power over, and status among, others is pertinent to the satisfaction of this need. One respondent, now in his seventies and active in Masonry for over fifty years, wrote that he believed the attraction of Masonry stems from the "desire to obtain the so-called secrets"; secondly, the measure of protection extended; third, and most important, the potential for the exercise of power given as a privilege to a select few: "As he aspires to advance in the order and applies himself to its working so that he can become Master (or some other presiding officer) he satisifies his desire of power to rule over his fellowman and his desire to feel superior. He has an opportunity to preside over his brother, something he has not obtained otherwise."[20] This gentleman, whose life encompasses major changes in the black experience in the United States, stressed the power aspect as more important than any other, both in the interview and in unsolicited letters. This is consistent with Max Weber's distinction of social honor as power and as a status dimension within stratification systems.[21]

The sense of belonging is confirmation rather than the initial conference of prestige. Those who possessed a measure of success in a specialized area appear to have been attracted to a more universally selective status group as confirmation at a higher level of their prowess and respectability.

---

an excellent treatment of the type and degree of Masonic, Catholic, and Mormon "subversiveness." In this research effort, the sole mention of antipathy toward nationwide black Freemasonry—and this is only one possible interpretation of the treatise—is Odum's 1910 discussion of white fear that black Masonic lodges were "hotbeds of vice" where "incendiary views are promoted." See his discussion on p. 140. Davis states: "Obviously the literature of countersubversion reflected concrete rivalries and conflicts of interest between competing groups, but it is important to note that the subversive bore no racial or ethnic stigma and was not even accused of inherent depravity" (p. 213).

20. Personal correspondence, June 1976.

21. Max Weber, *The Theory of Social and Economic Development,* pp 428–29. Suzanne Keller's concept of "strategic elites" similarly offers a suggestive interpretive framework for understanding Masonic members, as does the literature on interpersonal influence. See Keller, *Beyond the Ruling Class*; Elihu Katz and Paul Lazarsfeld, *Interpersonal Influence.*

Self-definition for a minority group is a particulary precarious issue; movement by some to emphasize symbols of status as buffers from criticism appears to be a logical adjustment.[22] Milton Gordon's concept of ethnic subsociety is suggestive for this interpretation since it highlights possibly valuable distinctions. Gordon specifies that there is a distinction between the group with which one identifies historically and the group that is the "locus of a sense of participational identification." With a person of the same social class but of a different ethnic group, one shares behavioral similarities but not a sense of peoplehood. With those of the same ethnic group but of a different social class, one shares the sense of peoplehood but not behavioral similarities.[23] Thus, the only group meeting both qualifications, offering a sense of historical identification as well as participational identification, is the group having the same ethnic and class location; in this case, the black middle-class achievers.

It is possible, as William Muraskin has argued, that some black males turned to Freemasonry to relieve ambivalence over negative feelings toward the black masses and a desire to dissociate oneself from them.[24] One can note at times an air of condescension toward the black masses, but since the literature of Freemasonry in general is paternalistic in tone toward those "unenlightened" by the craft, the thrust of the condescension is difficult to categorize. Prince Hall Freemasonry does provide a tightly knit social environment and lifestyle for those who are relatively more successful in their endeavors. By its nature, however, a secret society utilizes secrecy to engender a sense of unity among believers. The internal bonds are strengthened by secrecy over internal matters and sometimes over activity. But this in itself does not mean nonconcern with and for the nonmember.

An 1848 speech by Frederick Douglass would appear to question black Masonic involvement for the betterment of all. In speaking of the need for blacks to improve and elevate themselves with and without white assistance, Douglass spoke of the greater appeal of fraternal groups over civic advancement groups. He spoke of the ease with which a Masonic or Odd

22. See Karen Horney, *The Neurotic Personality of Our Time*, for a thorough treatment of the general issue of self-definition.
23. Milton Gordon, *Assimilation in American Life*.
24. William Muraskin, *Middle Class Blacks in a White Society*, p. 277.

Fellow gathering could draw attendance from the 500,000 or more free blacks at that time. A fraternal gathering in New York City, he said, drew between four and five thousand, while a gathering called to plan strategies for the emancipation of slaves would be lucky to draw fifty persons. The numbers are no doubt used rhetorically; but while it can be argued that a public meeting, well announced, might not be the best method to devise the nuances of liberation strategy, Douglass's points should be considered.

He saw the white interest in encouraging the involvement of blacks in the Odd Fellows, Masons, and so forth as a way of ensuring white security. Involvement in fraternal activities would drain energy from civil rights activities that were threatening to the white status quo. Douglass exhorted the audience:

> We are imitating the inferior qualities and examples of white men, and neglecting superior ones. We do not pretend that all members of oddfellow societies and masonic lodges are indifferent to their rights and the means of obtaining them; for we know the fact to be otherwise. Some of the best and brightest among us are numbered with those societies . . . We desire to see these noble men expending their time, talents and strength for higher and nobler objects than any that can be attained by the weak and glittering follies of oddfellowship and freemasonry.[25]

These works and their intent should be carefully examined in the light of the context of the times and the historical record. For one, overt action and covert action are not being distinguished. But what further evidence exists to disprove Douglass's charge against Freemasonry as channeling energy better spent on the advancement of the race? Was his intent rhetorical perhaps?

Earlier negative evaluations of the black bourgeoisie in the sociological literature are no doubt biased due to the limited amount of published research at that time concerning infragroup stratification patterns. Ira Berlin's 1974 publication, *Slaves Without Masters,* offers valuable new insight into the factors leading to a wide diversity of status levels and styles within the black middle class.[26] Berlin dissects the various splits within this

---

25. Frederick Douglass, "What Are Colored People Doing for Themselves?" *Negro Social and Political Thought,* p. 205.

26. The number of black upper-class elites has always been small. In speaking of the antebellum South, Berlin notes: "The elite communities

anomalous body, demonstrating the nuances of regional differences compounded with urban and rural differences that in turn were affected by degree of dependence upon the white economy, shade of skin complexion, religious practices, and so forth. He wrote:

> The color line between brown and black never rigidly followed class divisions. There were many poor mulattoes and a few wealthy blacks. In addition, denomination differences, distinctions between free Negroes who had enjoyed freedom for generations and those *nouveaux* who had but recently won their liberty, crisscrossed class and caste distinctions.[27]

Gunnar Myrdal, E. Franklin Frazier, and others did not have the advantage of this and other more modern forms of data collection. Biased extrapolations have been made to all of the black middle class based on characteristics and behavior symptomatic of smaller segments of the black population.

This study is not meant to deny the existence of conspicuous consumption socially. Groups displaying this behavior, however, can be more accurately described as subsections of either the older aristocracy, the black upper-class elites,[28] or the middle class. Thus, the valid question in analyzing black Freemasonry is the extent to which the career of the organization was responsible to the larger black community.

It is usually held that American Freemasonry is more broadly

---

varied in size from place to place, but they rarely amounted to more than 10 percent of the free Negro caste, and usually not even that. In some places a handful of families constituted the entire free Negro upper class." See Ira Berlin, *Slaves Without Masters: The Free Negro in the Antebellum South*, p. 282.

27. Ibid., p. 283.

28. In most European nations, Freemasonry had an up and down career; peace, followed by persecution, then peace again as Masonic beliefs in liberalism and individual conscience threatened particularly wary religious groups and ruling parties. European Masons were indeed reformers and revolutionaries in some instances. They represented in their communities the spirit of new cosmopolitan humanitarianism and rationalism. There is much literature debating the issue of a Masonic connection with the French Revolution, the Society of United Irishmen, the Philhellenic movement in Greece, and the Decembrist movement in Russia. See Norman MacKenzie, *Secret Societies*, and T. Desmond Williams, *Secret Societies in Ireland*, for a full discussion of this point. French Masonry in the late eighteenth century, for example, has been described as the "chief rallying point of many currents of

humanitarian toward nonmembers than the European brother-hood.[29] The data appear to suggest that Prince Hall Free-masonry has been the catalyst for societal reform. The African Masonic hall in Boston was a meeting place for the cause of abolition. Women were even allowed to speak out for abolition and against colonization efforts, a privilege not extended in most public gatherings. The ringing David Walker Appeal in 1830, perceived as an incendiary document advocating militant over-throw, was first presented following a dinner held at the Masonic Temple.[30]

Individual Masons and lodges were involved in the abolition movement. Thomas Dalton, for example, an active Prince Hall Mason, was the president of the Massachusetts General Colored Association in 1833, an abolitionist society.[31] The secret nature of the black Masonic organization in Washington, D. C., frightened slave interests and its supporters. In the early years, the lodge meetings came to be held on the banks of the Potomac River, a "reversion to a very ancient custom," because of the refusal of the city fathers to allow them to meet in their lodge halls. Known members were summoned before magistrates on one pretext or another. Curfew violations were often charged. The lodge was quite accurately suspected of being part of the "underground railroad" system.[32] In 1807, one-third of the

---

discontent, the center of organized propaganda for ideals which it did not create" (Frank H. Hankins, "Masonry," *Encyclopedia of the Social Sciences*, p. 183). In Russia, Freemasonry emerged among the aristocracy at the end of the eighteenth century. Czar Nicholas I censured Masonry for its alleged participation in the Decembrist uprising and the fellowship went under-ground until the 1860s. Mention is made of this in Leo Tolstoy's novel *War and Peace*. See also Henry C. Coil, W. R. Hervery, and Charles C. Hunt, "Masonic Fraternity," *Encyclopedia Americana*. Through a historical perspec-tive, it appears that European Masonic groups served as the "natural channel or framework" for the formation of change-oriented groupings (J. M. Roberts, *The Mythology of Secret Societies*, p. 295).

29. See Benjamin Quarles, *Black Abolitionists.* David Walker, a North Carolinian clothes dealer who settled in Boston, was active in the General Colored Association formed in 1826 for racial betterment and the abolition of slavery. Walker's seventy-six page militant call for retaliatory action stemmed from this group.

30. Harry E. Davis, *A History of Freemasonry Among Negroes in America*, p. 42.

31. Quarles, *Black Abolitionists*, p. 184.

32. *The Informer*, p. 3, July 1956.

blacks in Washington (about 1,500 persons) were free. A small group of the freedmen had established a school; it is this group that later founded the Washington, D. C., Prince Hall lodge in 1823, which was involved in transporting slaves to free territory.

A commemorative speech in 1956 rings with the sense of dedication of Prince Hall Masonic brethren:

> It was no mean legacy that was handed to us by the men who defied the edict of the Supreme Court of the United States in the 1850s that "no Negro has any right that a white man is bound to respect." These Negroes dared to organize Masonic lodges during the most anti-Negro period in the history of the state of Indiana and to oppose the stand of most political leaders for the colonization of Negroes outside the United States. Not only did they dare to organize Masonic Lodges, they also had to fight for the elementary rights of citizenship like public school education, the ballot, equality before the courts, and the right to hold property when the weight of public opinion in the state was against them. These early Masonic Brothers of ours had to beg, fight and beseech for the right to fight, for the preservation of the Union, in the Civil War. Our Grand Lodge went on record in 1862, a whole year before the State was persuaded to act, in favor of the employment of Negroes in the Army of the United States. After the color bar to enlistment was removed so many of the officers and members of the Prince Hall Lodges went into the Army that no Grand Lodge (in Indiana) could be held during the year 1864.[33]

This and similar data suggest that black Masons as individuals and as groups were integrally involved in community and state affairs. Some have said that the black lodges were "merely prefabricated Republican clubs" in the South during the Reconstruction years.[34] But involvement has extended throughout: the first black elected politicians in most states were Prince Hall Freemasons. Frazier has argued that black politicians have gained power by their associational membership in such fraternal organizations.[35]

33. Joel Williamson, *After Slavery: The Negro in South Carolina During Reconstruction*.

34. See E. Franklin Frazier, *Black Bourgeoisie*. This is consistent with Alvin J. Schmidt and Nicholas Babchuck, "The Unholy Brotherhood: Discrimination in Fraternal Orders," *Phylon*, and Williamson, *After Slavery*.

35. Miscellaneous papers in the Schomburg Collection; Charles H. Wesley, *The History of the Prince Hall Grand Lodges of Free and Accepted Masons of the State of Ohio 1849–1971*.

Black Masons have worked to stem the toll of racial atrocities. Up through the 1930s, black Masons worked to get the federal government to implement antilynching enforcement. In addition, indirect evidence that black Masons have been involved and accepted in the black community is that little antagonism has been expressed toward them by the community. Some clergy and laity did rail against the center of black life being shifted to the lodge. The supposed mixture of sinners and Christians in fraternal organizations was perceived by a few as leading to religious laxity.[36] Those countering this attitude spoke of the educational value of Masonic affiliation, stressing the emphasis on the civic virtues of honesty, diligence, and commitment to a truly humane society.

The lodge halls were frequently utilized by community groups for activities other than Masonic procedures. For example, in the early twentieth century, an Odd Fellows hall in Georgia was the original site of the Fort Valley State College of Georgia. Classes in reading and arithmetic were started for persons of all ages within the black community.[37] Black Masons have always been concerned with maintaining community responsibilities; committees within the lodge structure are delegated for "community relations." William Muraskin, who has recently indicted black Masons as being too bourgeois, ironically offers excellent examples of twentieth-century charismatic officials of subordinate and state lodges who were most outspoken in urging their constituency to act as concerned citizens for all measures and means of civil rights. A further indication of community concern can be seen in a 1929 anniversary notice of a subordinate lodge in Phoenix City, Alabama. In an invitation extended to other lodges and "race leaders," the lodge speaks of its service benefits: "The order is now helping race members to own homes and will erect a hospital for the race. We also pay the face value of policy to policy holders who become permanently disabled from blindness, paralysis, accidents or for any cause rendering one disabled so long as they live . . . Race members

36. See Howard W. Odum, *Social and Mental Traits of the Negro,* p. 138. One cannot help but recall the radio series, and early television program, "Amos and Andy," which, replete with stereotypes, created and projected the image of the lodge hall as a diversion for the men from nagging wives.

37. Donnie D. Bellamy, "Henry A. Hunt and Black Agricultural Leadership in the New South," *The Journal of Negro History,* pp. 464–79.

feel blessed to have a Masonic order under the title of the race."[38] The Masonic principle that a single rose for the living is better than a costly wreath for a grave is conducive to an activistic, community-oriented approach within Prince Hall Freemasonry throughout its history. Some Prince Hall lodges have built and maintained homes for the elderly. During the Depression years, many continued to attempt to hold fast to the tenets of "brotherly love, relief and truth," despite the vast unemployment and shaky financial grounding.[39]

Some of these service activities are for members and their families only. Blood banks in many lodges are an example of benefits to members and relatives only. Various actions are taken to look out for the interest of older members. The Massachusetts lodge, for example, waives the financial obligation for certain worthy individuals over the age of 65 who have been actively involved continuously for twenty-five years or more.[40] Lodge members attend and actively participate in funeral services for their deceased brethren or appoint a committee to function as a representative body for such an occasion. A donation is given to the widow of a deceased Prince Hall Mason. Several respondents told of elderly and isolated Masons, found by chance in nursing homes or institutions, who were adopted by the local lodges and extended Masonic friendship and privileges by different lodges rather than those of their initial participation. Various subordinate lodges have worked in conjunction with other civic associations for community betterment. Specific examples include guidance and leadership training programs in conjunction with the local Urban League, NAACP, or local civic group. Community-wide children's parties at holiday times are sometimes held by individual lodges.

In addition, one can note particular benefits and opportunities accruing to certain segments within the black middle class. The large number of businessmen is an example:

Many small businessmen have entered . . . because it has of-

38. Anniversary Notice, Sons of Solomon Lodge No. 88, Rising Star Lodge No. 92 of the Modern Free and Accepted Colored Masons of the World, Phoenix City, Alabama, 28 July 1929. Schomburg Collection.
39. See Wesley, *The History of the Prince Hall Grand Lodges,* chapter eleven.
40. Robert C. Garnett, Jr., compiler, *Proceedings of the Most Worshipful Prince Hall Grand Lodge,* p. 12.

fered the promise of increased patronage and aid; many more successful entrepreneurs, because it has provided an arena for the exercise of their skills and a vehicle for their more ambitious plans for racial uplife; and for large numbers of talented and frustrated non-businessmen it has provided a school for learning business skills and an opportunity for employing them in running both the fraternity itself and its many separate businesses.[41]

But focus upon the benefits generated solely for members and kin masks the impact upon the general black community. There has been, and is, noble precedent for the involvement of black Masons in the community. Black Masons are pragmatic for one must be flexible in all matters due to categorical societal definitions of black status.

Efforts for change within the community and society might not have been visibly evident on a consistent basis in each and every community, but they have taken place—in fact, and they still do. A constructive, pragmatic motivation of the Masons (and Elks, Odd Fellows, Greek sororities and fraternities, and so forth) has prompted them to not unnecessarily showcase their activities on behalf of the larger community until the most recent wave of legislated civil rights mandates.

A negative attitude toward the masses does not correlate with the history of the Prince Hall Masons. The confusion perhaps stems from the view of the black leadership class as synonymous with the black elite, or vice versa, and the lack of historical knowledge and awareness of the various levels of function of black groups and the middle class. The leaders are those who maintained ties with others, sharing the same problems facing all blacks. One often finds writers of the present speaking of the black middle class as neglectful of their lower-class racial brothers. On the basis of this study, one cannot accept such a broad generalization.

Community concerns are not a new phenomenon for black Masons. A factor partially contributing to the lack of awareness of black Masonic involvement has been the invisibility of the black press. Only recently have black media become abundant enough to report on any but major social affairs.[42] The fact that

41. Muraskin, *Middle Class Blacks,* p. 99.
42. The increase in publication and circulation of black periodicals in the late 1960s and 1970s has been phenomenal. Blacks have had less success

the black press has been overburdened by attempts to single-handedly report on black news because of the neglect of the mainstream press has not been fully considered by those condemning black middle-class persons. News of organizational endeavors has mainly circulated within the membership via word of mouth, newsletters, and magazines. Some of the printed materials sent solely to members are now part of the Schomburg collection on black Freemasonry. These document a genuine social consciousness that extends beyond the parameters of members and families.

There is a further, more basic fact of the black experience: it is only in the second half of the twentieth century that the larger society has looked with beneficence upon indications of black solidarity. Black gatherings have been viewed with suspicion well into modern times. If actual lodge meetings were considered dangerous, as they were for example in Maryland in 1870 when leading white citizens had the black King David Lodge No. 5 of Havre de Grace suppressed by arresting and fining its members,[43] then it is certain that goal-oriented action for change by black persons would be infinitely more threatening.

Overt action is increasingly visible as one approaches today's context. Black Masons are being urged to more fully realize their power in numbers in facing the challenge of the multitude of social problems in today's society. They are urged, however, to stay at the front line of change in a manner that is not divisive. Political endorsement of candidates and political agendas and programs are to be avoided. But concern and action for the obtainment of civil rights *is* considered consistent with Masonic principles and highly unlikely to cause division along party lines among blacks.

The wave of exhortation in recent years reflects the changing weltanschauung of black communities across the nation. While black protest has been the common experience, the form it has taken and the degree of visibility have been determined by pragmatic survival definitions. Overt action is increasingly the case given the perception by blacks of the large number of

---

with access to, and exposure in, broadcast media. The National Black News Network, the first nationwide minority news service, originated in 1972 to meet the need for both coverage of the black community and coverage of events and facts having consequences for minorities.

43. Davis, *History of Freemasonry*, p. 175.

power resources—numbers, commitment, mobilization mechanisms, communication channels, outside allies—available at this time.[44] But Prince Hall Masons have always been expected to be aware and active regarding the facts and consequences of the minority experience in America and the world. Thus it appears particularly erroneous to condemn Freemasonry among blacks as draining of energy or protest. Attempting to maintain middle-class identification is a practical aspiration. One cannot as easily exert effective influence upon any system from the lower classes. For Muraskin to castigate black Masonic leaders as antagonistic to poor blacks because of speeches recognizing the fact and problem of increased black crime and of failure to unify all blacks is fallacious reasoning. A more valid interpretation would suggest that the speechmakers were recognizing a genuine problem area that was getting out of hand, a fact documented by social scientists. The unity of a group, whether racial or class, is not easily accomplished, and the total accomplishment of this is beyond the power of any fellowship, religion, or ideology.

Despite repeated berating of the bourgeois nature of Prince Hall Freemasonry, even Muraskin notes that "Masonry has never offered a fantasy land of . . . escape from the racial problems that have afflicted their people in America."[45] The persistence of racism has prevented it on the one hand (Muraskin's contention); the lack of desire for either oblivious escape or full integration (my contention) is another.

The Shriners, for example, are committed to the principle of fostering economic and educational development and presently operationalize this commitment by contributions to educational and health-related institutions. They have also been cognizant and prideful of the moral obligation of Shriners to continue to struggle for full freedom for all. During the early years of the current era of civil rights activity, a black Shriners journal noted that all black Masonic temples would be observing a victory day celebration for a court decision that declared interstate-bus segregation illegal. All were to use the occasion to highlight the

44 Winthrop Jordan, *White Over Black: American Attitudes Toward the Negro, 1550–1812;* August Meier and Elliott Rudwick, *From Plantation to Ghetto.*

45. Muraskin, *Middle Class Blacks.*

many achievements blacks have made; blacks were to rejoice as the Jews did during their Passover period.[46]

Prince Hall Masons have been at the forefront of civil rights support. Masons in the North were urged in the early 1960s to renew their commitment:

> We as Prince Hall Masons, particularly in the North, should not stand idly by smug in the feeling that we are secure and safe from the conditions of oppression or segregation. To the contrary—where these conditions are specifically and definitely outlined or established in certain sectors of our country there is a more subtle or tactful application of the same conditions right here in our backyard. This type of action is more keenly felt than a open and overt act. It therefore behooves us to join forces with those attempting to eradicate these evils once and for all.[47]

Prince Hall Masons have made donations to groups such as the NAACP and its Legal Defense and Educational Fund, Inc., the Negro College Fund, and aid to local groups and scholarship funds. In 1951, the Prince Hall Masons legal research department was established to funnel contributions from lodges into litigation efforts. A half-million dollars are said to have been utilized for the Brown case fighting school segregation.[48] As one journal stated, a major objective of black Masons must be " to remove the unconstitutional barriers to the enjoyment of full Citizenship Rights by Negroes in America." The article, written at the height of Martin Luther King's nonviolent movement, noted the continuing support extended to the NAACP Legal Defense and Educational Fund, Inc.:

> In 1961– 1962, we supported the Honorable Thurgood Marshall, then Director Counsel of the NAACP Legal Defense as he began the Supreme Court Test Case on School Desegregation with $15,000; in 1964 this case came to a successful conclusion with a favorable Court decision which is now history. From 1951– 1961, Prince Hall Grand Lodge spent $250,000 in support of Civil Rights; 1961– 1962, $750,000;

46. *The Pyramid* (South Carolina Prince Hall Grand Lodge, 1946).
47. Vidal A. MacKinnon, *Proceedings of the Most Worshipful Prince Hall Grand Lodge,* Free and Accepted Masons of Massachusetts.
48. Muraskin, "Black Masons: The Role of Fraternal Orders in the Creation of a Middle-Class Black Community," Ph.D. diss., University of California-Berkeley, p. 204.

Rights then is not new and shall continue through research, education and Legal Redress.

. . . We presently have 124 separate actions now pending before the Supreme Court affecting 7,500 individuals, black and white alike, who through peaceful demonstrations have run afoul of the law. Our pledge in 1960 was to support and defend every non-violent demonstrator who requested our aid, and the policy remains in effect.[49]

Some lodges have used federal funds. The Ohio grand lodge moved in the late sixties to utilize federal funds made available in the Kennedy-Johnson era to underwrite their investment in low-income housing for senior citizens. Black Masons feel particular pride that one of their fellow Masons, Thurgood Marshall, a thirty-third degree Mason and Grand Minister of the State of the United Supreme Council, Southern Masonic Jurisdiction, Prince Hall Affiliation, sits on the Supreme Court.

There has been internal dissension, as would be expected in any large associational grouping. It has not, however, been out of proportion, as Muraskin contends by labeling Prince Hall Freemasonry as ineffectual due to anarchy and disrespect for its leaders.[50]

One major dissension among black Freemasons stemmed from a situation in Pennsylvania where Harmony Lodge No. 5 was expelled by the Prince Hall grand lodge for contumacy (disobedience). The members, a few years later in 1833, applied successfully to a white lodge in Norristown for a charter. Three subordinate lodges joined with the initial group as the Hiram Grand Lodge of Pennsylvania, which functioned for ten years as an outspoken rival of the Prince Hall lodges. In 1845, the white lodge that had supposedly granted the charter began to vigorously deny any such act or connection. Confusion and controversy raged. The grand master of the Prince Hall Grand Lodge of Massachusetts offered to mediate but this only increased the public uproar over the situation and slowed the eventual disbanding.[51]

A study of a small southern cotton-mill town uncovered another similar situation. There were twenty-three active black voluntary associations in the town with tensions existing be-

49. *The Lamp* (Ohio Prince Hall Grand Lodge, 1st Quarter, 1964).
50. Muraskin, *Middle Class Blacks,* p. 207.
51. For a full discussion of this situation, see Harold Van Buren Voorhis, *Negro Masonry in the United States,* chapter nine.

tween two Masonic lodges: one of Prince Hall affiliation and one independent clandestine group. Personal rivalry between two male leaders further heightened the tension. The Prince Hall lodge was ranked by the community members as having more prestige because of the greater selectivity of membership. The stability of an individual, as measured by his job and his steadiness at it and his reputation in the community, is of vital importance to Prince Hall Masonry. The upstart group saw the Prince Hall group as old, inactive, and, worst of all, elitist. The Prince Hall group, in turn, saw the upstarts as morally unscrupulous by virtue of their clandestine or unauthorized existence and leadership. Here, too the upstart group had its lodge established by a white lodge of Master Masons when the black grand lodge would not permit territorial duplication. The potential for dissension inherent in such actions by white Masonry may have been calculated, but no information exists to prove or disprove the matter. Both groups were in operation at the end of the study.[52]

The community status of Prince Hall Masons was also mentioned in the study. Being a Mason implied "distinctive status and behavioral standards," and implied a high degree of ethical behavior. Prince Hall Freemasonry was the only organization in the town whose aspirants worried to a great extent over their acceptance or rejection. The black Masons in the community had twice the membership of the Elks. The school, church, and lodge hall were all located together and somewhat interdependent, forming a focal center of the black community.

A more recent example of internal factionalization occurred over the building of a new temple. Various factions applauded and decried the intended commercial usage of portions of the building: the renting of the ballroom and certain other rooms to non-Masonic groups and affairs. The deputy grand marshall exhorted his fellow members to "join together in Brotherly Love to help and assist in the completion" of the new temple:

> We cannot enjoy the irrational reasoning of singular gains or glories, for only collectively can we reach the goals we have in view. We must continue to select leaders who can display and embrace the philosophy of who can best work and agree together in control. Our petty jealousies, dislikes and personal

52. Hylan Lewis, *Blackways of Kent.*

miffs must give way to the practice of Brotherly Love, Relief and Truth.[53]

Reports from various subordinate lodges noted the resurgence of interest in Freemasonry after the construction of the new edifice. Membership steadily increased in those lodges meeting in the new building, which is cited as vindication for the forces supporting the building and intended usage of the new temple. The presiding grand master noted with pleasure that despite the poor state of the national economy, and despite the specific status of blacks within the economy, Masonry was still attractive. It proves, he said, "that money is not the deciding factor whether or not a man joins the craft; I maintain that if we project the proper image the individual will want to fraternize with us."[54] The younger members praised themselves for their more innovative ways; the older members still had reservations about the new team way of doing things.

The examples of internal struggles within Prince Hall Masonry appear to be those common to large associations: dissension at times, but never anarchy. An examination of the black experience, as with any minority experience, must distinguish between statements that can best be categorized as declamatory in nature rather than definitive in purpose.

Prince Hall Freemasons remain a vital and viable part of the community infrastructure of black America. There is evidence that black Masonic involvement remains at a constant level. When questioned about the present attraction of Freemasonry to younger blacks, one respondent spoke of the greater attractiveness of Masonry on the local level now than at earlier times. He mentioned with pride that this was despite the fact that Masonry "promises you nothing"; the actions of Masons are enough to draw new members. This respondent, a Mason for over fifty years, had himself become attracted to Masonry by the image presented by his uncle and his uncle's friends. He recalled the impression made upon him by the sound of the gavel on his uncle's casket during the Masonic burial ceremonies. That incident propelled him to seek membership.

Some attention is paid to maintaining appeal for young male achievers. Prince Hall Masonic grand lodges have recently

53. Garnett, *Proceedings,* p. 18.
54. Ibid., p. 64.

sponsored Pythagorean groups for young high school males.[55] Scholarship benefits are attached to many of the youth groups. The Massachusetts grand lodge recently recommended that "as many Master Masons as possible become Fraternal Fathers to a number of Pythagoreans for one year for the purpose of giving spiritual and financial assistance to the future Masonic leaders." Another measure to ensure admittance of youths to the lodges was an advisory recommendation stemming from the 1970 gathering of all state grand masters[56] suggesting that the individual grand lodge consider amending their constitutions to allow initiation at age eighteen rather than twenty-one.[57] While this could be interpreted as part of the general societal trend toward lowering the age of responsibility, it is likely an attempt to smoothly move a youth involved in the more recreational aspects of Masonry into the order before he becomes otherwise involved outside Masonic circles. This does not mean that younger Masons are any less multi-affiliated than older Masons; it does mean an attempt to make Masonic attachment attractive in their formative years and predominant in individual rankings.

It is difficult to obtain a valid measure of the age range of the membership. From data collected from sparse documents and interviews the average age appears to be in the late forties. This was interpreted by respondents as a healthy sign of the spread of Freemasonry throughout adulthood. Given the fact that one works his way up the hierarchy over a period of years, the average does appear significant. The bank teller, the junior executive, the administrator, and others see the value, perhaps more instrumental than expressive, of maintaining Masonic ties with other blacks. One subordinate lodge in an eastern city appears to be composed mainly of persons in their thirties and forties. In this lodge, the initial fee to join twenty years ago was fifty dollars; the present fee is $175.

55. The name is taken from the Greek philosopher and athlete, Pythagoras. Drill teams and bands participate in local and regional competitions and at annual convention affairs.

56. Each grand lodge is autonomous. Within Prince Hall Freemasonry, a national grand lodge did exist for a while. It was an advisory council founded in 1847. Constant conflict over state versus subordinate autonomy led to its dissolution in 1877. See Harry A. Williamson, "Legitimacy of Negro Masonry," *National Fraternal Review*, p. 4. The gatherings now imply no formal advisory relationship.

57. Garnett, *Proceedings*, p. 11.

Public advertising is a recent, unusual phenomenon. The major black newspaper in a large midwestern city recently ran a two-column advertisement with a picture of a thirtyish, bearded man, name listed, stating: "International F. & A. M. Masons and Order of Eastern Stars are having a membership drive. We would like to welcome you into our family. You will have the opportunity to travel and have friends wherever you go. If you would like to join us phone . . ."[58]

Presently there are Prince Hall grand lodges in Canada, the Bahamas, the West Indies, Ethiopia, and Liberia. Additional lodges can be found at various American military bases throughout Europe. These traveling military lodges are primarily composed of Army and Air Force personnel and only rarely civilians at military installations. For example, a recent state-level Annual Communication carried a recommendation to grant a dispensation to allow a group of Master Masons, now part of Traveler's Lodge No. 25, Bitenberg, Germany, to form a separate lodge in the Netherlands. This was recommened because of the four and one-half hours traveling time from Soesterberg, Holland, for lodge attendance by sixteen members of the German lodge. The various Traveler's lodges organize Masonic study clubs among "young, intelligent military (mostly officers) personnel."[59]

Traditional American values are interwoven into the Masonic ambience. Owning property, a prevalent ideal in American society, has been a major goal of Masons individually and collectively. Rather than viewing this emphasis negatively, as Muraskin has, one must understand the functional aspect of such ownership for a minority group. Owning one's own home, land, or group site signifies achievement in our class-stratified society.

Further, the data refuted Muraskin's contention that the Masonic order functioned to teach the previously unknown "bougeois social role with which they have had limited or no prior experience."[60] The black middle class must not be assumed to be a culturally or educationally deprived grouping. Males in this stratum have achieved some measure of occupational and community standing prior to their move toward Freemasonry. The minority Masons, in all instances, are achievers bringing

58. *St. Louis Argus,* 4–11 May 1978.
59. Ibid., p. 25.
60. Muraskin, *Middle Class Blacks,* pp. 49–50.

attitudes and skills required in the organizational processes and procedures. The lodge room and activities serve as vehicles to exercise mannerliness and brotherhood, traditionally seen as humanistic characteristics inculcated in black children by religious-oriented, as well as survival-oriented, parents. Black Masons have held fast to the American dream, realizing fully the gap between the dream and the reality. Over the years various state and subordinate bodies have issued patriotic statements in support of various war efforts and fought to become a part of, or gain better status within, the military.

To summarize, Prince Hall Freemasonry has been demonstrated to serve multiple functions. It provided or provides: travel security in a new community (vital during slavery and segregation in this society); security of a social network; assurance of association with like-minded individuals facing similar situations; recognition of status in this lifetime and at death; a sense of order in worldview; a place for orderly progression via specific achievements; the setting for reinforcement of positive self-image; experience in legal and business procedures; experience in public speaking and decisionmaking; a chance to make a difference in community affairs. It will be interesting to follow the direction Prince Hall Freemasonry takes as black leadership faces the challenge of moving beyond its major emphasis on legal endeavors for social equity to increased participation in those public policy positions implementing and enforcing action for a just society.

Chapter 11

Implications of Pillarization

Prince Hall Freemasonry remains today the mirror image of white Freemasonry. The black Masons have, however, acted upon the internalized service role in differing ways and are increasingly cognizant of the actual and potential power of their organizational unity and autonomy. The history of Prince Hall Freemasonry provides suggestive insight into the general phenomenon of separate, parallel organizational forms deeply rooted within the black community. The persistence of parallel institutions, once maintained by coercion but increasingly by choice, is a strong reality of the black community. While a racial minority group may have visible physical and subcultural differences, albeit segmented, it, like the dominant group or groups, is subject to similar societal and cultural influences. The black experience has been shaped by the white experience, and vice versa; the relationship is reciprocal.[1] Thus, many values, aspirations, behavioral tendencies, and so forth are the same or similar in nature.

One might have expected status ladders to be different in the black and white social world. Much of the recent social science literature on the black experience would seem to indicate support for that type of hypothesis. However, it is clear that the major accoutrements of black, African-oriented institutions in the United States today are relatively new phenomena of the past two decades.[2] No evidence has been found of any unique

1. See part four of Daniel J. Boorstin, *The Americans: The National Experience.* Boorstin argues that the unique characteristic of America stems from the very necessary possibility that something better will appear as Americans search for community. For Boorstin, American civilization is a by-product of this constant search. The validity of this interpretation of the black experience is documented in Albert Murray's *The Omni-Americans.* For a more theoretical treatment of the growth of group experiences, see L. Singer, "Ethnogenesis and Negro Americans Today," *Social Research,* pp. 419–32.

2. See Orlando Patterson, *Toward a Future That Has No Past.* Also see

African influence, or particular Africanisms, in the ritual and operating procedures of black Freemasonry.[3] The economic, political, and social power of an Anglo-settled society made it the model for adjustment forms for minority groups in the United States.

Minority responses exhibit the subtlety and complexity of power contexts.[4] Basic to the power theory of Max Weber is the premise that human beings are status-seeking creatures and that positive status and power are inextricably intertwined. It is here argued that membership in a pillarized organization, one paralleling a valued institution in mainstream society, has been perceived by minorities as a potential resource of status and power.

Whether an item qualifies as a power resource is determined by consideration of the objectives surrounding the use of the item. For a minority-group member, participating in a parallel organization has had pragmatic value and, most importantly, being at the forefront of positive change seems to have been a more pertinent motivating factor toward the institutional form of Freemasonry than the need for status-inconsistent persons to rally together for insulation purposes.

Black Freemasonry has been influential in the establishment of guarantees for greater freedoms for blacks in the United States and elsewhere. It has been demonstrated that black Ma-

---

Harold Isaacs, *The New World of Negro Americans,* on the historical pattern of American black attitudes toward Africa.

3. Though often challenged, Melville J. Herskovitz's *The Myth of the Negro Past* remains the most important work on African cultural influence on black Americans. Most social scientists now accept evaluative and expressive components as the sole survivals in relatively original form. Kingsley, an authority on West African societies, attempted unsuccessfully to compare tribal societies to American associations such as Freemasonry. See Hutton Webster, *Secret Societies,* p. 126. This is consistent with earlier research conducted by Guy B. Johnson, "Some Factors in the Development of Negro Social Institutions in the United States," *American Journal of Sociology,* pp. 329–37; Edward N. Palmer, "Negro Secret Societies," *Social Forces,* pp. 207–12. However, it must be remembered that universal Freemasonry acknowledges the importance of Africans in that Egypt is venerated as the source of the principles and as the teachers of Grecian and Roman civilizations. Thus, there is a spurious connection for universal Freemasonry. See David C. Pick and G. Norman Knight, *The Pocket History of Freemasonry.*

4. See Hubert M. Blalock, Jr., *Toward a Theory of Minority Group Relations.*

sons have not docilely accepted the status quo. This parallel organization, by virtue of its relative innocuous content and its mystique of power, could and did serve in some measure as a vehicle for change. It would be accurate to speak of Prince Hall Masons as progressive, welcoming and aiding orderly change. With legal strides for blacks finally materializing, black Freemasonry has become increasingly confident of its latent potential and is now attempting to exercise its power to a greater extent and more visible manner in the wider society.[5]

By focusing upon Freemasonry, we have examined the process of pillarization by race in the United States that has occurred in this particular organization. We have seen that autonomy has come to be the prime concern of the black Masonic actors. What are the implications of the coexistence of structurally and ideologically identical institutions separated along racial lines?

Autonomy, self-independence, and alternatives have long been the goals of the majority of black Americans, as they have been for most rational human beings. The structural manifestations of this in black social institutions, and the biracial nature of many societal institutions, need to be carefully examined. The importance of a continuous tradition for American blacks and, by inference, other minority groups, has not been fully discussed by social scientists. A sense of the continuity of a people is often articulated in discussions of the increasing politicization of ethnicity; it has universally existed throughout time.[6] Throughout most of the American black experience, the maximum time and effort have been spent on establishing legal procedures for the dismantling of the rigid structure of Jim Crow laws, institutions, and practices.[7] Now that this structure

5. Richard T. Watkins, in his article "Black Social Order: Expanding Their Goals to Fit the Needs of the Community at Large," *Black Enterprise,* pp. 26– 29, notes that all black civic and social groups are visibly engaged in endeavors for community betterment. While all these groups have consistently donated large financial resources to civil rights organizations, only now are they receiving media coverage of their national attempts. This article is particularly focused upon the actions of the black sororities and fraternities.

6. The problem at various times has been to decide who constituted the people. Boundary parameters rather than continuity of tradition have been the issue.

7. See Charles V. Hamilton, "The Crisis of Black Political Participation," *The Public Interest,* pp. 188– 210.

has begun to crumble and gigantic, although insufficient, strides have been made in erecting barriers to help prevent its reemergence, white and black liberals seem uneasy with the importance of black institutions to the black collectivity. A recent article discussing Dr. Carter G. Woodson, esteemed black historian stated:

> The belief upon which Carter G. Woodson staked his manhood, his single-minded life effort, was that black people had a toughly resilient yet broad tradition which could be a refuge in times of trouble, inspiration in times of doubt, and foundation for new progress in times of precarious confidence. For holding fast to the conviction that blacks must independently develop a continuous tradition, Woodson was styled a propagandist by uncomprehending whites, and opposed by some blacks as an intellectual separatist at a time when a premium was placed on interracial organization.[8]

It is this same misunderstanding or miscomprehension that confronts us today when social scientists speak of integration or separation as a dichotomy instead of a linear dimension, or fail to analytically distinguish between cultural pluralism as a concept of fluid choice and separatism as a concept of rigidity.

Taking the matter back further in terms of sociological analysis, distortion or confusion may stem in part from preoccupation with caste as an explanatory model for black-white relations. The caste model is most useful for the analysis of segregated American society; it is less useful for today's situation of more fluid race relations. Thus, the pillarization model is suggested here as an analytical tool.

A horizontally segregated or caste system by definition involves a degree of interdependence between birth-ascribed groupings; a vertically separated or pillarized form involves interdependence among associational groups and a measure of fluidity. Pillarization implies choice. In a horizontally segregated system, every individual belongs to a clearly specified caste and there is no overlap in membership. The dominant group defines the nature of all relationships. This no longer describes the

---

8. Michael R. Winston, "Carter Godwin Woodson: Prophet of a Black Tradition," *The Journal of Negro History,* p. 462. Woodson rose from poverty to attain his doctorate from Harvard at the turn of the twentieth century. He founded the prestigious *Journal of Negro History,* the Association for the Study of Negro Life and History, and was the originator of annual observances of Negro or Black History Week.

United States; nor does individual assimilation describe the totality of the contemporary trend in American race relations. As we have seen in this case history, emulation of ideals and assimilation in interactions can and must be analytically distinguished as distinct processes differing in goals and consequences.

The social costs of caste are multifold: intergroup violence, exploitation, and the waste of human resources. What are the social costs of contemporary pillarization? This examination of Prince Hall Freemasonry suggests that vertically parallel organizations serve the function of validating both social recognition and social worth. They emerged from the struggle of minority groups to become economically and socially self-sufficient in an alien or threatening community,[9] and have remained in their incomparable ability to bolster the maintenance of pride and esteem by offering a familiar and fixed reality. Conclusions about black society resulting from "retarded assimilation" cannot be upheld.[10] Nor can these data be taken as proof of the complete ideal of acculturation of large segments of the black population. The premise of white society as the ideal is the crucial point of difference. It has been demonstrated that black Freemasonry was less an imitation of the mainstream organization than a striving to catch up with the status and position of mainstream America via an organization that symbolized noble principles and noble actions by responsible leaders of the community. If acculturation within the sociological literature of race relations could be transposed to mean the "American society hodge-podge," Prince Hall Freemasonry would then be an indication of black acculturation to the larger society with the explicit reservation of an individual's right to choose with whom one wants primary affiliation.

Just as differences emerged when moving the caste model from a religious area to that of race, so differences emerge when transposing the concept of pillarization from a religious model in one country, the Netherlands, to a racial model in another.

9. Edna Bonacich, "A Theory of Middleman Minorities," *American Sociological Review*, pp. 583–94, argues that communal solidarity emerges among middlemen minorities which leads to preferential allocation of resources (credit, information, and so forth). This in turn leads to outsiders viewing the group as clannish and disloyal.
10. See, for example, Oliver C. Cox, *Caste, Class and Race.*

However, the identification and comparison of similar institutional structures may lead to fruitful insights into conditions, concomitants, and consequences. The concept of pillarization seems useful as an analytic tool for contemporary society for several reasons:

1. It removes the dichotomous connotations inherent in the caste concept, replacing it with a continuous, linear concept of degree of pillarization.
2. It suggests a greater degree of pluralistic autonomy; the sharing of power and prestige potential is inherent.
3. It blunts differential ranking by moving from birth-ascription toward consensual choice.
4. A flexible degree of mutual enforcement is suggested.
5. It, unlike caste, is methodologically quantifiable since degree of pillarization in a social system is of a continuous nature.

One can examine racially pillarized institutional developments as indicators of the strength of ethnic communities rather than as negative indicators of the residue of segregation.

Although an aggravated state of relations does presently exist between blacks and whites, the issue of minority responses is too complex to be seen as accommodation and imitation or rebellion and alienation alone. While notions of political separatism do exist among small segments of the black population, the majority seeks some form of equitable incorporation within the changing society. Speaking of integration versus separation as a dichotomy is misleading. Not only are the relative proportions of advocates massively distorted in the public perception but the reality of day-by-day relations is overlooked.

Many have been wary of qualifying integration. For example, Frederick Douglass warned early of the dangers he saw as inherent in establishing pillarized institutions. He urged blacks to protest discriminatory practices in white churches where blacks were seated separately and ministered to unequally. He urged blacks to force the churches to live up to their ideals by sit-ins and other nonviolent protest tactics. Douglass warned that "complexional distinctions" in both religious and social institutions would only further compound misunderstanding between white and black and would also lead to further inequality. The warning is still heard today.[11] However, these institu-

11. See, for example, Bayard Rustin, "Ethnics: A New Separatism," *AFL-CIO Federationist,* pp. 8–11.

tions exist in viable form and appear in this age of militant ethnicity to be functional for the development of greater autonomy and equality of meaningful opportunity.

In the case of black Freemasonry, despite doctrinal mandate of abstinence from political protest, one can perceive that Masonic leaders are maintaining community commitment and, in fact, are escalating this to new visible levels. Only by detailed analysis of other such racially pillarized institutions can the autonomy potential of pillarization be assessed. If collective self-consciousness moves to an effectively organized coalition stage, these pillarized institutions of the black community could be a major force of benefit in the structuring of our society in a harmonious fashion. Pillarization worked well in the Dutch situation where Catholics and Calvinists maintained their separate educational institutions, and when the lower class, because of heavy concentration in one of the pillarized groupings, gained the right to vote. The case of contemporary Ireland as a religious caste system that has failed to make the move to effective pillarization, unlike the past situation in the Netherlands, may recommend this concept beyond the Dutch society.

Clearly more research is necessary to isolate the crucial variables involved in the pillarization process to assess whether enclosure or autonomy is the more likely consequence. Operationalization of the concept may lead to methodological problems because indicators must be developed for each factor, their statistical properties assessed and assigned, and crude indices developed and refined. However, the probable utility of this conceptualization for systematic analysis of modes of minority adaptation merits consideration by scholars.

Perhaps segmented or vertical integration will be the normative reality for the United States in the future. If collective black self-consciousness moves to an effectively organized coalition stage, the black pillarized institutions could be a major force in the structuring of our society. Much discussion has occurred in sociological circles about how sociologists were caught shorthanded in predicting the past quarter-century of American race relations. While much work has resulted from this aroused or chagrined awareness, pillarization may be a viable concept to explore in an attempt to meet the new round of questions being raised by heightened ethnic consciousness among all segments of the American population and to facilitate improvement of intergroup relations.

Appendix

Methodology

Developing a research protocol for this study was a challenging task, complicated by three factors: the two-hundred-year history, the subject of interest being black, and the nature of the organization under focus. This researcher found, as have many other researchers, that in focusing upon the history of the black American experience from the minority perspective itself, traditional approaches to historical analysis are impossible. There is an across-the-board paucity of written records for experiences in the black community whether one is interested in individuals or in organizations.

Continuity is difficult to trace when examining a secret society—now, admittedly, more a society having secrets than a secret society—such as Prince Hall Freemasonry over a two-hundred-year period. The individual lodges rarely kept records, minutes, or any written materials; the material in those that did was frequently only name lists or Masonic lore. Moralistic sermonettes and historical firsts comprise the major substance.

An editorial in a 1954 Prince Hall state journal, *The Informer*, states the difficulty in obtaining and verifying information on black Freemasonry. Although the writer is speaking of the situation in his state, it can easily be generalized. First he cites the paucity of black newspapers, then the secrecy of the Masons themselves:

> It must be and it must have been then that the Negroes who took the obligation of Masonry were under the impression that they were never to reveal anything no matter how unrelated to the secrets of Masonry. The secrecy of the Masons of other days has robbed the historian of many good sources of information just as the secrecy of those of the present day robs the editor of valuable news material and complicates the work of future historians of our order. And many lodges still follow the practice initiated by these pioneer lodges in allowing the secretary when he leaves office to take with him as his personal property the records which have accumulated during his tenure of

office. . . . An outside researcher has difficulty finding evidence of action even though Masons have always done significant things.

As the writer notes, it is only recently—the last two decades in particular—that the small but persistent black press has been able to broaden the coverage of the black experience. Books concerning the black experience, presently increasing in number, have tended to have a moralistic or judicial goal in mind. Hortatory declamation must be carefully evaluated. Personal memoirs and oral interviews have provided useful information. Thus, the data utilized for this study are an interpretive amalgam of printed materials, remnants and reminiscences, and self-reported opinions of past and present members, and secondary sources, some of which are becoming standards in the growing volume of research into the black experience. Intriguing and revealing aspects of black life often become apparent by asking new questions of standard material.

Techniques from oral history methodology were utilized. Only recently have American social scientists begun to appreciate the potential in such techniques. Africanist Jan Vansina presents an interesting discussion of this point: "Africans chide us for hurrying, for not lingering over an oral communication to savor its bouquet, to meditate about it, to make it part of one's intellectual personality, rather the way one savors poetry."[1] Interviews with present-day Masons, particularly the long-time members, proved abundantly fruitful. Many spent long periods of time expressing their views and memories. Being a female was a definite asset in the open-ended interviews of these black males. Many were courtly in assisting this researcher to understand the "intricacies" of the male organization. While most mentioned the women's auxiliaries, few thought that these would be of interest to me; or, it might also be said, few thought that these were on the same level of import or interest as the male lodges![2] At this time, being black and female should

1. Jan Vansina, "Once Upon a Time: Traditions as History in Africa, *Daedalus*, p. 442.
2. The first Black Eastern Star chapter, the women's affiliate in Freemasonry, was formed in North Carolina in 1880. In mainstream Freemasonry, the first women's group was founded in 1867. This symbolic group does not have the same range of degree differentiation as the male body but does have a hierarchy of officers and positions. It initially spread

perhaps be added to the list of sociological "unobtrusive measures"! Often the researcher was introduced to new source persons and material as a result of a conversation and passed on with approval within a social network.

Finding indicators of activity was difficult. Both faith and action within the Masonic belief system cannot be easily quantified for statistical analysis. For the adherent, Freemasonry is a belief system and worldview that does not necessitate quantification, measurement, or basically any written record. The secrecy of Masonry for a believer bespeaks serious commitment. It is acknowledged that the objects and principles of Freemasonry are now public, but the ceremonials, intitiation, and so forth are supposedly kept secret. Noel P. Gist's comprehensive study of fraternalism proved useful in this regard. It is one of the very few treatments building upon Georg Simmel's seminal monograph, "The Secret and the Secret Society."

All sociohistorical analyses must stand up to careful scrutiny on several levels. Has the right question been raised? Have all interpretations been explored in developing valid explanations? What types of sources have been used and for what reasons? What types of sources have others working in similar areas utilized and for what reasons? What have been the past findings regarding the phenomenon under study? Have they been adequately summarized and mined for utility in the present analysis? The search for social and historical accuracy is elusive and often unattainable, but it has been attempted in this research effort. By a process of triangulation, perhaps the closest validation can and did occur. By comparing and contrasting direct and indirect accounts of what occurred, the reality constructs of individuals alive and dead, factual information and commonalities began to emerge. Enough material was available to ascertain whether Freemasonry was an avenue for or reinforcer of social mobility for the male achievers of a minority population. From the lodge records and papers, one can establish some basic

---

through the southern states, through the west, and now is found in all parts of the United States. The Heroines of Jericho is another black Masonic affiliate. Its membership is drawn from the wives, mothers, sisters, and daughters of Royal Arch Masons in good standing. The Heroines of Jericho, found in 31 jurisdictions (29 states, Liberia, and the Bahamas), determines its own goals and is particularly active in service capacities within the community.

understanding of the outlook of the respective Masonic bodies, their concerns and actions. Quite naturally, the records present greatest insight into the leaders of the particular lodges and state bodies, but the Masonic lodge proliferated and circulated ranks and duties to allow fuller participation of its members.

The interpretive approach was interdisciplinary: historical, economic, political, and psychological factors were incorporated in the sociological analysis. Doing sociology, for this researcher, involves systematic study of social interaction, structure, and their consequences, manifest and latent. Researching Prince Hall Freemasonry required a great measure of sociological detective work. While one can perceive this as a weakness of the analysis, it is my argument that overcoming these barriers increased resourcefulness and imaginative competence, which in turn honed the focus and quality of the study. Thus, maximum use of documents, formal and personal, verbal interchanges, literary sources, and so forth were utilized to focus on the development of an organization, its structure, processes, and maintenance.

While wide-ranging extrapolation cannot be made on the basis of this one case study, it is hoped that suggestive avenues of approach emerged that can be utilized for a series of studies of various institutions within a minority community. Given the nature of a social science as cumulative, it is my hope that this study may stimulate other examinations of pillarized institutions and societies.

Selected Bibliography

Adorno, Theodore W. *The Authoritarian Personality.* New York: Harper and Row, 1950.

Allport, Gordon. *Becoming: Basic Considerations for a Psychology of Personality.* New Haven: Yale University Press, 1955.

Bacote, Henry. *Who's Who Among the Colored Baptists.* Kansas City: Franklin Hudson Publishing Company, 1913.

Bailyn, Bernard. *The Ideological Origins of the American Revolution.* Cambridge: Harvard University Press, 1967.

Baker, Ray Stannard. *Following the Color Line.* 2d rev. ed. New York: Harper and Row, 1964.

Bell, F. A. *Order of the Eastern Star.* Chicago: Ezra Cook, 1956.

Berger, Peter. *The Noise of Solemn Assemblies.* Garden City: Doubleday, 1961.

Berlin, Ira. *Slaves Without Masters: The Free Negro in the Antebellum South.* New York: Pantheon Books, 1974.

Berreman, Gerald D. "Caste as Social Process." In *Ethnic Conflicts and Power,* edited by Donald E. Gelfand and Russell D. Less, pp. 33– 47. New York: John Wiley and Sons, 1973.

Blackwell, James E. *The Black Community: Diversity and Unity.* New York: Dodd, Mead and Company, 1975.

Blalock, Hubert M., Jr. *Toward a Theory of Minority Group Relations.* New York: John Wiley and Sons, 1967.

Blumer, Herbert. *Symbolic Interactionism: Perspective & Method.* Englewood Cliffs: Prentice-Hall, 1969.

Boorstin, Daniel J. *The Americans: The National Experience.* New York: Vintage Books, 1965.

Boris, Joseph J. *Who's Who in Colored America,* vol. 1. New York: Who's Who in Colored America Corp., 1927.

Boulware, Marcus. *The Oratory of Negro Leaders 1900–1968.* Westport: Negro Universities Press, 1969.

Brawley, Benjamin. *Social History of the American Negro.* New York: Macmillan, 1921.

Brinton, Crane C. *The Anatomy of Revolution.* New York: Random House, 1957.

Brooks, Juanita. "On the Mormon Frontier, the Diary of Hosea Stout," vol. 2, 1848– 1861, MS, n.d.

Brotz, Howard. *Negro Social and Political Thought.* New York: Basic Books, 1968.

Bruce, John Edward. *Prince Hall, the Pioneer of Negro Masonry.* New York: n.p., 1921.

Caldwell, John D. *New Day—New Duty.* Ohio: n.p., 1876.

Cartwright, Dorwin, ed. *Studies in Social Power.* Ann Arbor: University of Michigan Press, 1959.

Cass, Donn A. *Negro Freemasonry and Segregation.* Chicago: Ezra Cook, 1957.

Centers, Richard. *The Psychology of Social Classes.* Princeton: Princeton University Press, 1949.

Chalmers, David M. *Hood Americanism: The First Century of the Ku Klux Klan 1865–1965.* New York: Doubleday, 1965.

Chesneaux, Jean. *Peasant Revolts in China 1840–1949.* New York: Norton, 1973.

Chicago Commission on Race Relations. *The Negro in Chicago: A Study of Race Relations and a Race Riot.* Chicago: University of Chicago Press, 1922.

Cox, Harvey. *The Seduction of the Spirit: The Use and Misuse of People's Religion.* New York: Harper and Row, 1973.

Cox, Oliver. *Caste, Class and Race.* New York: Monthly Review Press, 1948.

Crawford, George W. *Prince Hall and His Followers: Being A Monograph on the Legitimacy of Negro Masonry.* New York: Crisis, 1914.

Cross, Whitney. *The Burned-Over District: The Social and Intellectual History of Enthusiastic Religion in Western New York 1800–1850.* New York: Harper and Row, 1950.

Dabney, Wendell P. *Cincinnati's Colored Citizens.* Cincinnati: Dabney, 1926.

Dai, Bingham. "Minority Group Membership and Personality Development." In *Race Relations: Problems and Theory,* edited by Jitsuichi Masuoka and Preston Valien, pp. 181–99. Chapel Hill: University of North Carolina Press, 1961.

Dann, Martin E. *The Black Press, 1827–1890: The Quest for National Identity.* New York: G. P. Putnam's Sons, 1971.

Davis, Harry E. *A History of Freemasonry Among Negroes in America.* United Supreme Council, Ancient and Accepted Scottish Rite of Freemasonry, Northern Jurisdiction, USA, 1946.

Degler, Carl N. *Out of Our Past: The Forces That Shaped Modern America.* New York: Harper and Row, 1959.

Delaney, Martin. *The Origins and Objects of Ancient Freemasonry: Its Introduction into the United States and Legitimacy Among Colored Men.* Pittsburgh, 1853.

Denslow, Ray V. *Regular, Irregular, and Clandestine Grand Lodges: A*

Bibliography

Study in Foreign Recognitions. Washington: The Masonic Service Association, 1956.

————. *The Masonic World by Ray Denslow*. Edited by Lewis C. Cook. Missouri Lodge of Research, 1964.

Denslow, William R. *Freemasonry and the American Indian*. The Masonic Service Association, 1956.

Deutsch, Morton and Krauss, Robert M. *Theories in Social Psychology*. New York: Basic Books, 1965.

Dewar, James. *The Unlocked Secret: Freemasonry Examined*. London: William Kimber, 1966.

Dollard, John. *Caste and Class in a Southern Town*. 3rd ed. Garden City: Doubleday, 1957.

Donald, Henderson H. *The Negro Freedman: Life Conditions of the American Negro in the Early Years After Emancipation*. New York: Schuman's, 1952.

Douglass, Frederick. "What Are the Colored People Doing for Themselves?" In *Negro Social and Political Thought*, edited by Howard Brotz. New York: Basic Books, 1968.

Drake, St. Clair and Cayton, Horace. *Black Metropolis*. New York: Harper and Row, 1945.

Du Bois, W. E. B. *The Philadelphia Negro: A Social Study*. New York: Schocken Books, 1967.

Durkheim, Emile. *The Elementary Forms of Religious Life*. New York: Collier, 1961.

Eliade, Mircea. *Rites and Symbols of Initiation*. New York: Harper and Row, 1958.

Epstein, Cynthia F. *Woman's Place*. Berkeley: University of California Press, 1974.

Factor, Robert L. *The Black Response to America*. Reading, Pa.: Addison-Wesley, 1970.

Ferguson, Charles W. *Fifty Million Brothers*. New York: Farrar & Rinehart, 1937.

Festinger, Leon. *A Theory of Cognitive Dissonance*. Evanston: Harper, Row & Peterson, 1957.

Franklin, John Hope. *The Free Negro in North Carolina, 1790–1860*. Chapel Hill: University of North Carolina Press, 1943.

————. *From Slavery to Freedom: A History of American Negroes*. New York: Alfred A. Knopf, 1947.

Frazier, E. Franklin. *Black Bourgeoisie*. Glencoe: Free Press, 1957.

————. "La Bourgeosie Noire." In *The Black Sociologists: The First Half Century*, edited by John H. Bracey, Jr., August Meier, and Elliott Rudwick. Belmont: Wadsworth Publishing Co., 1971.

Fromm, Erich. *Man for Himself*. New York: Rinehart and Co., 1945.

141

————. *The Revolution of Hope: Toward a Humanized Technology.* New York: Harper and Row, 1968.

Genovese, Eugene D. *Roll, Jordan, Roll.* New York: Pantheon Books, 1974.

George, Carol V. R. *Segregated Sabbaths.* London: Oxford University Press, 1959.

Goffman, Erving. *The Presentation of Self in Everyday Life.* New York: Doubleday, 1959.

Goldmann, Lucien. *The Human Sciences and Philosophy.* Translated by Hayden White and Robert Ancha. London: Cape, 1969.

Gordon, Milton. *Assimilation in American Life.* New York: Oxford University Press, 1964.

Goudsblom, Johan. *Dutch Society.* New York: Random House, 1968.

Greene, Lorenzo J. *The Negro in Colonial New England.* New York: Atheneum Publishers, 1969.

Grimshaw, William H. *Official History of Freemasonry Among the Colored People in North America.* Montreal: Broadway, 1903.

Hage, Jerald. *Techniques and Problems of Theory Construction in Sociology.* New York: John Wiley and Sons, 1972.

Hannah, Walton. *Darkness Visible: A Revelation and Interpretation of Freemasonry.* London: Britons Publishers, 1961.

Hare, Nathan. *The Black Anglo-Saxons.* London: Collier-Macmillan, 1965.

Hawke, David. *The Colonial Experience.* New York: The Bobbs-Merrill Co., 1966.

Hechter, Michael. *Internal Colonialism.* Berkeley: University of California Press, 1975.

Herskovitz, Melville J. *The American Negro.* New York: Alfred A. Knopf, 1929.

————. *The Myth of the Negro Past.* Boston: Beacon Press, 1958.

Highan, John. *Strangers in the Land: Patterns of American Nativism 1860–1925.* New Brunswick: Rutgers University Press, 1955.

Hill, Roy L. *Who's Who in the American Negro Press.* Dallas: Royal, 1960.

Horney, Karen. *The Neurotic Personality of Our Time.* New York: W. W. Norton and Co., 1947.

Hughes, Everett C. and Hughes, Helen. *Where Peoples Meet: Racial and Ethnic Frontiers.* Glencoe: Free Press, 1952.

Huizinga, Johan. *Homo Ludens.* London: Routledge and Kegan Paul, 1949.

Isaacs, Harold R. *The New World of Negro Americans.* Cambridge: Harvard University Press, 1963.

Bibliography

Jackson, Luther P. *Free Negro Labor and Property Holding in Virginia, 1830–1860.* New York: Appleton-Century Company, 1942.

Johnson, Melvin M. *The Beginnings of Freemasonry in America.* New York: George H. Doran and Co., 1924.

Johnson, Robert B. "Negro Reaction to Minority Group Status." In *American Minorities,* edited by Milton Barron, pp. 192–212. New York: Alfred A. Knopf, 1957.

Jordan, Winthrop. *White Over Black: American Attitudes Toward the Negro, 1550–1812.* Baltimore: Penguin Books, 1968.

Kardiner, Abram, and Ovesey, L. *The Mark of Oppression.* New York: W. W. Norton and Co., 1950.

Katz, Elihu, and Lazarsfeld, Paul. *Interpersonal Influence.* Glencoe: Free Press, 1955.

Katz, Jacob. *Jews and Freemasons in Europe, 1723–1939.* Cambridge: Harvard University Press, 1970.

Keller, Suzanne. *Beyond the Ruling Class.* New York: Random House, 1963.

Kelley, H. H. "Two Functions of Reference Groups." In *Readings in Social Psychology,* rev. ed., edited by Theodore M. Newcomb and Eugene L. Hartely, pp. 40–105. New York: Holt and Company, 1952.

Kurokawa, Minako. *Minority Responses.* New York: Random House, 1970.

Lenski, Gerhard E. *Power and Privilege.* New York: McGraw-Hill, 1966.

Lewin, Kurt. *Resolving Social Conflicts: Selected Papers on Group Dynamics.* New York: Harper and Row, 1948.

Lewis, Hylan. *Blackways of Kent.* Chapel Hill: University of North Carolina Press, 1955.

Lijphart, Arend. *The Politics of Accommodation: Pluralism and Democracy in the Netherlands.* Berkeley: University of California. Press, 1968.

Lipset, Seymour M., Trow, Martin, and Coleman, James. *Union Democracy.* Garden City: Anchor, 1956.

Little, Kenneth. *West African Urbanization: A Study of Voluntary Associations in Social Change.* Cambridge: Cambridge University Press, 1965.

Litwack, Leon F. *North of Slavery: The Negro in the Free States, 1790–1860.* Chicago: University of Chicago Press, 1961.

Lowie, Robert H. *Social Organization.* New York: Holt, Rinehart and Winston, 1963.

Luckmann, Thomas. *The Invisible Religion.* New York: Macmillan, 1967.

MacKenzie, Norman. *Secret Societies.* New York: Collier, 1967.

Mackey, Albert G. *Encyclopedia of Freemasonry and Kindred Sciences.* Masonic History Company, 1887.

McManus, Edgar J. *Black Bondage in the North.* Syracuse: Syracuse University Press, 1973.

McWilliams, Wilson Carey. *The Idea of Fraternity in America.* Berkeley: University of California Press, 1973.

Manning, Frank E. *Black Clubs in Bermuda: Ethnography of a Play World.* Ithaca: Cornell University Press, 1973.

Maslow, Abraham H. *Motivation and Personality.* New York: Harper and Row, 1970.

Mather, Frank L. *Who's Who of the Colored Race,* vol. 1. Memento Edition. Half Century Anniversary of Negro Freedom in U.S. Chicago, 1915.

Mead, George Herbert. *Mind, Self and Society.* Chicago: University of Chicago Press, 1934.

Mecklin, John Moffatt. *The Ku Klux Klan: A Study of the American Mind.* New York: Harcourt, Brace and Company, 1924.

Meier, August, and Rudwick, Elliott. *From Plantation to Ghetto.* New York: Hill and Wang, 1970.

Merton, Robert K. and Rossi, Alice. "Contributions to the Theory of Reference Group Behavior." In *Social Theory and Social Structure,* edited by Robert K. Merton. Glencoe: Free Press, 1957.

Miller, Kelly. *Race Adjustment: Essays on the Negro in America.* New York: Walter Neale, 1910.

—————. "Radicals and Conservatives." In *Radicals and Conservatives and Other Essays on the Negro in America,* edited by Kelly Miller, pp. 25–41. New York: Schocken Books, 1968.

Muraskin, William A. *Middle Class Blacks in a White Society: Prince Hall Freemasonry in America.* Berkeley: University of California Press, 1975.

Murray, Albert. *The Omni-Americans.* New York: Outerbridge and Dienstfrey, 1970.

Myrdal, Gunnar. *An American Dilemma.* New York: Harper and Row, 1944.

Northrup, Soloman. *Twelve Years a Slave.* New York: Dever, 1970.

O'Dea, Thomas. *The Mormons.* Chicago: University of Chicago Press, 1957.

Odum, Howard W. *Social and Mental Traits of the Negro.* New York: AMS Press, 1966.

Otto, Rudolf. *The Idea of the Holy.* London: Oxford University Press, 1958.

Park, Robert Ezra. *Race and Culture.* Glencoe: Free Press, 1950.

Patterson, Orlando. *Ethnic Chauvinism: The Reactionary Impulse.* New York: Stein and Day Publishers, 1977.

Pettigrew, Thomas F. *Racially Separate or Together?* New York: McGraw-Hill, 1971.

Pick, Fred L. and Knight, G. Norman. *The Pocket History of Freemasonry.* Trowbridge: Redwood, 1971.

Pitt, David C. *Using Historical Sources in Anthropology and Sociology.* New York: Holt, Rinehart and Winston, 1972.

Quarles, Benjamin. *Black Abolitionists.* New York: Oxford University Press, 1969.

Ratner, Lorman. *AntiMasonry: The Crusade and the Party.* Englewood Cliffs: Prentice-Hall, 1969.

Redding, Saunders. *They Came in Chains.* New York: J. B. Lippincott Company, 1950.

Roberts, J. M. *The Mythology of the Secret Societies.* London: Seeker and Warburg, 1972.

Rosenberg, Morris. *Society and the Adolescent Self-Image.* Princeton: Princeton University Press, 1965.

Ross, Edyth L. *Black Heritage in Social Welfare: 1860–1930.* Metuchen, N. J.: Scarecrow Press, 1978.

Runciman, W. G. *Relative Deprivation and Social Justice.* London: Rutledge and Kegan Paul, 1966.

Russell, John H. *The Free Negro in Virginia.* New York: Dover Publications, 1969.

Schermerhorn, R. A. *Comparative Ethnic Relations.* New York: Random House, 1970.

Schmitt, Raymond. *The Reference Other Orientation: An Extension of the Reference Group Concept.* Carbondale: Southern Illinois University Press, 1974.

Sherif, Muzafer, and Sherif, Carolyn. *Reference Groups.* New York: Harper and Row, 1964.

Shibutani, Tamotsu. *Society and Personality: An Interactionist Approach to Social Psychology.* Englewood Cliffs: Prentice-Hall, 1961.

Shibutani, Tamotsu, and Kwan, Kian M. *Ethnic Stratification: A Comparative Approach.* New York: Macmillan, 1965.

Shils, Edward. *The Torment of Secrecy.* New York: Free Press, 1956.

Simmel, Georg. "The Secret and the Secret Society." In *The Sociology of Georg Simmel,* edited and translated by Kurt H. Wolff, pp. 307–76. Glencoe: Free Press, 1950.

———. *On Individuality and Social Forms,* edited by Donald N. Levine. Chicago: University of Chicago Press, 1971.

Simmons, Rev. William J. *Men of Mark: Eminent, Progressive and Rising.* New York: Arno Reprint of 1887 edition, 1968.

Slaughter, Linda Warfel. *Freedom of the South.* New York: Kraus Reprint, 1969.

Smith, Constance, and Freedman, Anne. *Voluntary Association: Perspectives on the Literature.* Cambridge: Harvard University Press, 1972.

Sorokin, Pitirim. *Social Mobility.* New York: Harper and Row, 1927.

Spear, Allan H. *Black Chicago: The Making of a Negro Ghetto, 1890–1920.* Chicago: University of Chicago Press, 1967.

Still, William. *The Underground Railroad.* Philadelphia: Proter and Coates, 1872.

Stillson, Henry L., and Hughan, William J., eds., *History of the Ancient and Honorable Fraternity of Free and Accepted Masons and Concordant Orders.* Boston: Fraternity Publishing Company, 1891.

Stinchcombe, Arthur L. "Social Structure and Organizations." In *Handbook of Organizations,* edited by James E. March. Chicago: Rand McNally & Co., 1965.

Stone, William L. *Letters on Masonry and Anti-Masonry Addressed to the Honorable John Quincy Adams.* New York: Halsted, 1832.

Sullivan, Harry Stack. *The Interpersonal Theory of Psychiatry.* New York: W. W. Norton and Company, 1953.

Tanner, Jerald and Tanner, Sandra. *Mormonism: Shadow or Reality?* Salt Lake City: Modern Microfilm Company, 1972.

Thomas, Emory M. *The Confederacy as a Revolutionary Experience.* Englewood Cliffs: Prentice-Hall, 1971.

Tiger, Lionel. *Men in Groups.* London: Panther, 1971.

Toch, Hans. *The Social Psychology of Social Movements.* Indianapolis: Bobbs-Merrill Co., 1965.

Tocqueville, Alexis de. *Democracy in America.* New York: Doubleday, 1969.

Tournier, Paul. *Secrets.* Richmond: Alfred A. Knopf, 1965.

Trelease, Allen A. *White Terror: The Ku Klux Klan Conspiracy & Southern Reconstruction.* New York: Harper and Row, 1971.

van den Berghe, Pierre L. *Race and Racism: A Comparative Perspective.* New York: John Wiley and Sons, 1967.

Van Deventer, Fred. *Parade to Glory.* New York: Pyramid Publications, 1964.

Voorhis, Harold Van Buren. *Negro Masonry in the United States.* New York: Henry Emerson, 1949.

———. *Our Colored Brethren: The Story of Alpha Lodge of New Jersey.* New York: Henry Emerson, 1960.

Bibliography

Waite, Arthur E. *The Secret Tradition in Freemasonry.* New York: E. P. Dutton and Co., 1937.

Wallerstein, Immanuel. *The World System.* New York: Academic Press, 1973.

Walton, Hanes. *Black Republicans: The Politics of the Black and Tans.* Metuchen, N. J.: Scarecrow Press, 1975.

Warner, W. Lloyd. *New Haven Negroes: A Social History.* New Haven: Yale University Press, 1940.

———. *Social Class in America.* Chicago: University of Chicago Press, 1949.

———. *American Life: Dream or Reality.* Chicago: University of Chicago Press, 1953.

Warren, Donald I. *Black Neighborhoods: An Assessment of Community Power.* Ann Arbor: University of Michigan Press, 1975.

Washington, Booker T. *The Story of the Negro: The Rise of the Race from Slavery.* New York: Doubleday, 1909.

Webb, E. J. *Unobtrusive Measures.* Skokie, Ill.: Rand McNally, 1966.

Weber, Max. *The Theory of Social and Economic Development.* New York: Free Press, 1947.

Webster, Hutton. *Secret Societies.* New York: Macmillan, 1908.

———. *Primitive Secret Societies.* New York: Macmillan, 1932.

Weiss, Robert S. "Materials for a Theory of Social Relations." In *Interpersonal Dynamics,* edited by Warren Bennis, Edgar Schein, Fred Steele, and David Barlow, pp. 154–63. Homewood, Ill.: Dorsey Press, 1968.

Wesley, Charles H. *History of the Improved Benevolent and Protective Order of Elks of the World.* Washington: The Association for the Study of Negro Life and History, Inc., 1955.

———. *History of Sigma Pi Phi: First of the Negro-American Greek Letter Fraternities.* Washington: The Association for the Study of Negro Life and History, Inc., 1954.

———. *Neglected History: Essays in Negro American History by a College President.* Washington: The Association for the Study of Negro Life and History, Inc., 1969.

———. *The History of the Prince Hall Grand Lodge of Free and Accepted Masons of the State of Ohio 1849–1971.* Washington: The Association for the Study of Negro Life and History, Inc., 1961.

———. *Prince Hall: Life and Legacy.* Philadelphia: Afro-American Historical and Cultural Museum, 1977.

Williams, T. Desmond. *Secret Societies in Ireland.* Dublin: Gill and Macmillan, 1973.

Williams, Robin M., Jr. *The Reduction of Intergroup Tensions: A Survey of Research on Problems of Ethnic, Racial and Religious Group Relations.* New York: Social Science Research Council, 1947.

Williamson, Harry A. *A History of Freemasonry Among the American Negroes.* New York: Macoy Publishing, 1929.

Williamson, Joel. *After Slavery: The Negro in South Carolina During Reconstruction.* Chapel Hill: University of North Carolina Press, 1965.

Wilson, Colin. *Religion and the Rebel.* London: Gollanez, 1957.

Wilson, William J. *Power, Racism and Privilege.* New York: Macmillan, 1973.

————. *The Declining Significance of Race.* Chicago: University of Chicago Press, 1978.

Woodson, Carter G. *The Negro Professional Man.* Washington: Association for the Study of Negro Life and History, 1934.

Woodward, C. Vann. *The Strange Career of Jim Crow.* New York: Oxford University Press, 1957.

Wright, R. R., Jr. *Who's Who in the General Conference 1924.* Philadelphia: *The Christian Recorder,* An African Methodist Episcopal Church, 1924.

Yenser, Thomas, ed. *Who's Who in Colored America.* 6th ed. Brooklyn: Yenser, 1944.

Yinger, J. Milton. *Religion, Society and the Individual.* New York: Macmillan, 1957.

Young, Frank W. *Initiation Ceremonies: A Cross-Cultural Study of Status Dramatization.* New York: Bobbs-Merrill Co., 1965.

Fraternal Journals

The Informer, Official Organ of PHGL of Indiana, F. & A. M., vol. 6–11 (1953–1958); vol. 12 (1958–1959).

The Lamp, Official Organ of MWPHGL of Ohio, F. & A. M., vols. 9–10 (1964–1965); vols. 3–4 (1960–1961); vols. 5–7 (1962–1963).

National Fraternal Review, Official Organ of the MWPHGL, F. & A. Masons of Illinois, May 1924 to September 1928 (monthly; inclusive with exception of June and July 1928), 1935.

Prince Hall Masonic Review, MWPHGL, F. & A. M., Jurisdiction of Georgia, vol. 1, no. 1, October 1937.

The Pyramid, Official Organ of the Imperial Council, Ancient Egyptian Arabic Order Nobles of the Mystic Shrine of North and South America and Jurisdiction. Organized 1893, Chicago, Illinois. Published quarterly. Buffalo, New York. 1946, 1956, 1966.

The Trestle Board, Official Organ of the N. W. Stringerbrand Lodge,

Bibliography

F. & A. M. and the Grand High Court, Heroines of Jericho, State of Missouri, Clarksdale. 1949, 1951, 1953.

West Virginia Masonic Bulletin, F. & A. M., 1953–1956, 1957–1958, 1960, 1963–1965.

The Royal Arch Mason, F. & A. M., vol. 9, Spring 1967, no. 1.

The Bee Hive of the Most Worshipful Grand Lodge, Ancient Free and Accepted Masons (Prince Hall Affiliation), Jurisdiction of Virginia. Lynchburg, Virginia. 1959, 1964.

Notice, Sons of Solomon Lodge No. 88, Rising Star Lodge No. 92 of the Modern Free and Accepted Colored Masons of the World, Phoenix City, Alabama, 28 July 1929.

Brochure, Prince Hall Public School Dedication, Gratz Street and Godfrey Avenue, Philadelphia, 21 September 1973.

Prince Hall Craftsman, vol. 12, no. 11, Spring-Summer, Fall 1973.

Articles, Manuscripts, Pamphlets

Adamson, J. H. "The Treasure of the Widow's Son." MS, n.d.

African Society. "The Laws of the Sons of the African Society Instituted at Boston, Mass., 1798." Boston, 1802.

Anderson, Robert. "Voluntary Associations in History," *American Anthropologist* 73 (February 1971): 209–22.

Babchuk, Nicholas, and Thompson, Ralph V. "The Voluntary Association of Negroes." *American Sociological Review* 27 (October 1962): 647–55.

Banton, Michael. *International Encyclopedia of the Social Sciences*, vol. 16, s.v. "Voluntary Associations: Anthropological Aspects," pp. 317–62. New York: Macmillan, 1968.

Bell, Howard H. "Free Negroes of the North 1830–1835: A Study in National Cooperation." *The Journal of Negro Education* 26:4 (Fall 1957): 201–9.

Bellamy, Donnie D. "Henry A. Hunt and Black Agricultural Leadership in the New South." *The Journal of Negro History* 40 (October 1975): 464–79.

Bennett, Lerone, Jr. "Pioneers in Protest: Prince Hall." *Ebony* 19 (April 1964): 89.

———. "The Black Pioneer Period." *Ebony* 25 (1970): 46–55.

Benoit-Smullyan, Emile. "Status, Status Types and Status Interrelations." *American Sociological Review* 9 (February 1944): 151–61.

Bierstedt, Robert. "An Analysis of Social Power." *American Sociological Review* 15 (December 1950): 730–38.

Black Chronicle. Simulated edition of a mythical 1794 paper. Boston: Blackside, Inc., 1971, no. 2.

Blassingame, John W. "Before the Ghetto: The Making of the Black

Community in Savannah, Georgia, 1865– 1880." *Journal of Social History* 6:4 (Summer 1973): 463– 88.

Blauner, Robert. "Marxian Theory and Race Relations." Paper presented at American Sociological Association meetings (August 1972).

Blumer, Herbert. "Race Prejudice as a Sense of Group Position." *Pacific Sociological Review* 1 (Spring 1958): 3– 7.

Bonacich, Edna. "A Theory of Middleman Minorities." *American Sociological Review* 38 (October 1975): 583– 94.

Breton, Raymond J. "Ethnic Communities and the Personal Relations of Immigrants." Ph.D. diss., The Johns Hopkins University, 1961.

Brown, Harvey N. *Freemasonry Among Negroes and Whites in America.* MS. Berlin Lodge, No. 46, F. & A. M., Rhode Island Constitution, 1965.

Butler, H. R. *History of Masonry Among Colored Men in Georgia.* Grand Master of Georgia, 1911.

Butts, Randall. "A New School Named 'Prince Hall.' " M. W. Prince Hall Grand Lodge of Pennsylvania (Fall 1973): 8– 9.

Clark, Peter B., and Wilson, James Q. "Incentive Systems: A Theory of Organizations." *Administrative Science Quarterly* 6 (September 1961): 129– 66.

Cohen, Abner. "The Politics of Ritual Secrecy." *Man* 6:3 (1971): 427– 47.

Coil, Henry C., Hervery, W. R., and Hunt, Charles C. *Encyclopedia Americana,* s.v. "Masonic Fraternity," pp. 383– 89b. New York: Americana, 1958.

Commission on Information for Recognition of the Conference of Grand Masters of Masons in North America. *Grand Lodge Recognition: A Symposium on the Condition of Grand Lodge Recognition.* New York: Macoy, 1958.

Crawford, George W. *The Prince Hall Counsellor: A Manual of Guidance Designed to Aid Those Combatting Clandestine Freemasonry.* Prince Hall Grand Masters Conference: n.p., 1965.

Dahl, Robert. "The Concept of Power." *Behavioral Science* 2 (July 1957): 201– 18.

Davis, David Brian. "Some Themes of Counter-Subversion: An Analysis of Anti-Masonic, Anti-Catholic, and Anti-Mormon Literature." *Mississippi Valley Historical Review* 48 (1960): 205– 23.

Davis, Harry E. "Documents Relating to Negro Masonry in America." *Journal of Negro History* 21:4 (1936): 411– 32.

———. "The Scottish Rite in the Prince Hall Fraternity." The United Supreme Council, Ancient and Affiliated Scottish Rite, 1940.

Drury, Rev. M. S. "Secrecy and Its Relation to the Family, State and Church." Address before the Iowa Anti-Secrecy Association, 26 April 1876. Chicago: Ezra Cook, 1876.

Eisenstadt, S. N. "Studies in Reference Group Behavior: I. Reference Norms and the Social Structure." *Human Relations* 7 (1954): 191–216.

Festinger, Leon. "A Theory of Social Comparison Processes." *Human Relations* 7 (1954): 117–40.

Fitchett, E. Horace. "The Origin and Growth of the Free Negro Population of Charleston, South Carolina." *Journal of Negro History* 26 (October 1941): 421–37.

Foote, Nelson N. "Identification as the Basis for a Theory of Motivation." *American Sociological Review* 16 (1951):14–21.

Fox, Sherwood. "Voluntary Associations and Social Structure." Ph.D. diss., Harvard University, 1952.

Frazier, E. Franklin. "Recreation & Amusement Among American Negroes." Carnegie Myrdal Papers, Schomburg Collection, New York Public Library, 1940.

Freeman, Howard E., Novak, Edwin, and Reeder, Leo G. "Correlates of Membership in Voluntary Associations." *American Sociological Review* 22 (October 1957): 528–33.

Garnett, Robert C., Jr., comp. *Proceedings of the Most Worshipful Prince Hall Grand Lodge*. Free and Accepted Masons located at Boston. 180th Annual Communication (1971) and 1st Semi-Annual Communication.

———. *Proceedings of the Most Worshipful Prince Hall Grand Lodge*. Free and Accepted Masons located at Boston. 181st Annual Communication, 1973.

Geschwender, James A. "Status Inconsistency, Social Isolation and Social Unrest." *Social Forces* 46 (1968): 477–83.

Gist, Noel P. "Secret Societies: A Cultural Study of Fraternalism in the United States." *The University of Missouri Studies* 15:4 (October 1940):1–184.

Glenn, Norval D. "Negro Prestige Criteria: A Case Study of Bases of Prestige." *American Journal of Sociology* 68 (May 1963): 645–57.

Goldberg, Milton M. "A Qualification of the Marginal Man Theory." *American Sociological Review* 6 (February 1941): 52–58.

Green, Arnold W. "A Re-Examination of the Marginal Man Concept." *Social Forces* (October 1947): 167–71.

Greene, Jack P. "Search for Identity: An Interpretation of the Meaning of Selected Patterns of Social Response in Eighteenth-Century America." *Journal of Social History* 3:3 (1970): 189–220.

Greene, Lorenzo J. "Prince Hall: Massachusetts Leader in Crisis." *Freedomways* 1:3 (Fall 1961): 238–58.

Hamilton, Charles V. "Blacks and the Crisis in Political Participation." *The Public Interest* 34 (Winter 1974): 188–210.

Hankins, Frank H. *Encyclopedia of the Social Sciences,* vol. 10, s.v. "Masonry," pp. 177–184. New York: Macmillan, 1935.

Hayden, Lewis. "Caste Among Masons." Address before Prince Hall Grand Lodge of Free and Accepted Masons of the State of Massachusetts, at the Festival of St. John the Evangelist, 27 December 1865. Boston: E. S. Commbs Co., 1865.

————. "Masonry Among Colored Men in Massachusetts." To the Right Worshipful J. G. Findel, Honorary Grand Master of the Prince Hall Grand Lodge and General Representative thereof to the Lodges Upon the Continent of Europe. Boston: E. S. Commbs Co., 1871.

Hazelrigg, Lawrence. "A Reexamination of Simmel's 'The Secret and the Secret Society': Nine Propositions." *Social Forces* 47:3 (March 1969): 323–29.

Henderson, C. R. "The Place and Function of Voluntary Associations." *American Journal of Sociology* 1 (November 1895): 327–34.

Himes, J. S. "Forty Years of Negro Life in Columbus, Ohio, 1900–1940." *Journal of Negro History* 2 (April 1942): 133–56.

Holden, David E. "Associations as Reference Groups: An Approach to the Problem" *Rural Sociology* 30:1 (March 1968): 63–74.

Horton, James E. "New Directions for Research in Black History." *The Black Scholar* 7:6 (March 1976):36–39.

Hughes, Everett C. "Social Change and Status Protest: An Essay on the Marginal Man." *Phylon* 10 (First Quarter 1949): 58–65.

Hyman, Herbert. "The Psychology of Status." *Archives of Psychology* 38 (June 1942): 269.

Jackson, E. F. "Status Consistency and Symptoms of Stress." *American Sociological Review* 27 (1962): 469–79.

Johnson, Rev. F. H. *Masonry, Past, Present, and Future Proved by Tradition, History and Revelation Including Two Hundred and Seventy-five Evidences that Masonry and Religion are the Same.* Buffalo, 1871.

Johnson, Guy B. "Some Factors in the Development of Negro Social Institutions in the United States." *American Journal of Sociology* 40 (1934): 329–37.

Johnson, Lois Q. "Voluntary Associations: A Study of Status Behavior." Master's thesis, Atlanta University, 1952.

Lassiter, Arthur B., Jr. *Proceedings of the Most Worshipful Prince Hall*

Bibliography

Grand Lodge. Free and Accepted Masons of Massachusetts located at Boston. 176th Annual Communication, 1967.

Lenski, Gerhard E. "Status Crystallization: A Non-Vertical Dimension of Social Status." *American Sociological Review* 19 (1954): 405– 13.

Levesque, George A. "Inherent Reformers—Inherited Orthodoxy: Black Baptists in Boston, 1800– 1873." *The Journal of Negro History* 40:4 (October 1975): 491– 519.

Litwack, Leon F. "The Federal Government and the Free Negro, 1790– 1860." *The Journal of Negro History* 43 (October 1958): 261– 78.

Lorwin, Val R. "Segmented Pluralism: Ideological Cleavages and Political Cohesion in the Smaller European Democracies." *Comparative Politics* 3:2 (1971): 141– 75.

Lowry, Ritchie R. "Toward a Sociology of Secrecy and Security Systems." *Social Problems* 19:4 (Spring 1972): 437– 50.

Ludendorff, Erich. *Destruction of Freemasonry Through Revelations of Their Secrets.* Translated by J. Elisabeth Koester. Paehl, Bavaria, 1957.

Lyman, Stanford M. "Chinese Secret Societies in the Occident: Notes and Suggestions for Research in the Sociology of Secrecy." *Canadian Review of Sociology and Anthropology* 1:2 (May 1964): 79– 102.

McDonagh, Edward C. "Status: A Human Form of Trapism." *Sociology and Social Research* (January-February 1960): 172– 77.

MacKinnon, Vidal A., comp. *Proceedings of the Most Worshipful Prince Hall Grand Lodge.* Free and Accepted Masons of Massachusetts located at Boston. 169th Annual Communication, 1960.

————. *Proceedings of the Most Worshipful Prince Hall Grand Lodge.* Free and Accepted Masons of Massachusetts located at Boston. 171st Annual Communication, 1962.

Manasse, Ernst. "Max Weber on Race." *Social Research* 14 (June 1949): 191– 221.

————. "Masonic Report Upholds 'Prince Hall Affiliation'." *Christian Science Monitor* (13 March 1977): 12.

Meier, August M. "Negro Racial Thought in the Age of Booker T. Washington, 1880– 1915." Ph.D. diss., Columbia University, 1957.

Miller, Nathan. *Encyclopedia of Social Sciences,* s.v. "Secret Societies," pp. 621– 23. New York: Macmillan, 1935.

Moberg, David O. "Religion and Society in the Netherlands and in America." *American Quarterly* 13 (1961): 172– 78.

Muraskin, William A. "Black Masons: The Role of Fraternal Orders in the Creation of a Middle-Class Black Community." Ph.D. diss., University of California-Berkeley, 1970; Ann Arbor, Michigan: University Microfilms.

"Nation's First Black-Owned TV Station to Begin Airing." *Jet Magazine* (24 July 1975): 24.

Norton, Mary Beth. "The Fate of Some Black Loyalists of the American Revolution." *The Journal of Negro History,* 58:4 (October 1973): 404– 26.

Olsen, Marvin. "Social and Political Participation of Blacks." *American Sociological Review* 35 (August 1970): 682– 97.

Orum, Anthony. "A Reappraisal of the Social and Political Participation of Negroes." *American Journal of Sociology* 72: 1 (July 1966): 32– 46.

Palmer, Edward N. "Negro Secret Societies." *Social Forces* 23 (December 1944): 207– 12.

Patterson, Orlando. "Toward a Future That Has No Past— Reflections on the Fate of Blacks in the Americas." *The Public Interest* 27 (Spring 1972): 25– 62.

Roberts, J. M. "Freemasonry: Possibilities of a Neglected Topic." *English Historical Review* 84 (April 1969): 323– 25.

Roy, Thomas S., ed. *Information for Recognition: Reports on Grand Lodges in Other Countries.* New York: Macoy, 1958.

Rugg, Henry W., ed. *The Freemasons' Repository,* vol. 17. Providence: Freeman, 1887– 1888.

Schlesinger, Arthur. "Biography of a Nation of Joiners." *American Historical Review* 1 (October 1944): 1– 25.

Schmidt, Alvin J., and Babchuck, Nicholas. "The Unholy Brotherhood: Discrimination in Fraternal Orders." *Phylon* 34: 3(1973): 275– 82.

Schomburg, Arthur A. "Freemasonry Versus 'An Inferior Race': Rejoinder Made to Recent Article by One Who Speaks for Negro Masonry." Harry A. Williamson Collection, Schomburg Library. n.p., n.d.

Schram, Stuart R. "Mao Tse-tung and Secret Societies." *China Quarterly* 27 (1966): 1– 13.

Seeman, Melvin. "Intellectual Perspectives and Adjustment to Minority Status." *Social Problems* 3 (January 1956): 142– 53.

"Segregation in Brotherhood." *Negro History Bulletin* 33 (October 1970; 132– 33.

Shepard, Silas H. "An Invaluable Bibliography: Notes on the Literature Dealing with Negro Freemasonry." *National Trestle Board* (March-April 1922): 68– 73.

Bibliography

Shibutani, Tamotsu. "Reference Groups as Perspectives." *American Journal of Sociology* 40: 6 (1955): 562–69.

Sills, David. *International Encyclopedia of the Social Sciences,* vol. 16, s.v. "Voluntary Associations, pp. 362–79. New York: Macmillan, 1968.

Singer, L. "Ethnogenesis and Negro Americans Today." *Social Research* 29 (1962): 419–32.

"65,000 Shriners Gather in New Orleans for 82nd Confab." *Jet Magazine* (9 October 1975): 19.

Stevens, Walter J. "Masonic Literature." *Alexander's Magazine* 1:12 (April 1906): 22–24.

Tiryakian, Edward A. "Toward the Sociology of Esoteric Culture." *American Journal of Sociology* 78:3 (November 1972): 491–512.

Traub, Stuart H. "Secrecy as an Elemental Sociological Form." Paper presented at the New York Sociological Association meetings, October 1973.

Twombly, Robert C., and Moore, Robert H. "Black Puritan: The Negro in Seventeenth-Century Massachusetts." *William and Mary Quarterly* 3rd series, 24:2 (April 1967): 224–42.

Upton, William H. "Light on a Dark Subject, Being a Critical Examination of Objective to the Legitimacy of the Masonry Existing Among the Negroes of America." Seattle: *The Pacific Mason,* 1889.

Vanden Zanden, James. "The Klan Revival." *American Journal of Sociology* 65:5 (March 1960): 456–62.

Vansina, Jan. "Once Upon a Time: Oral Traditions as History in Africa." *Daedalus* (Spring 1971): 21–42.

Wakeman, Joel. "A Sermon on the Nature and Tendencies of Secret Societies." Delivered at Prattsburg, New York, on 25 January 1847. Prattsburg: Palmer, 1847.

Watkins, Richard T. "Black Social Order: Expanding Their Goals to Fit the Needs of the Community at Large." *Black Enterprise* (July 1975):26–29.

Williams, Loretta J. "The Social Psychology of Secret Societies." MS, 1975.

———. "Pillarization as an Analytic Tool in Race Relations." Paper presented at the Society for the Study of Social Problems, San Francisco, 1975.

Williamson, Harry A. *Negroes and Freemasonry.* MS. Harry A. Williamson Collection, Schomberg Research Center, New York Public Library, 1923.

———. "Legitimacy of Negro Masonry." *National Fraternal Review* (May 1924): 3–5.

————. "The Position of Negro Masonry." *National Trestle Board,* n.p., n.d.

————. "A Square Deal." *National Fraternal Review* (September 1925): 2–5.

————. "Prince Hall or Negro Masonry." *The Masonic Analyst,* Harry A. Williamson Collection, Schomburg Research Center, New York Public Library, n.d.

Wilson, William J. "Ethnic and Class Stratification: Their Interrelation and Political Consequences—North America." Paper presented at 8th World Congress, August 1974.

Winston, Michael R. "Carter Godwin Woodson: Prophet of a Black Tradition." *Journal of Negro History* (October 1975): 459–63.

Wittermans, Tamme, and Krauss, Irving. "Structural Marginality and Social Worth." *Sociology and Social Research* 48 (April 1964): 348–60.

Wooten, Cleo. "Historical Sketch." MS. Boston, Massachusetts, 1951.

Yancey, William L., Ericksen, Eugene P., and Juliani, Richard N. "Emergent Ethnicity: A Review and Reformulation." *American Sociological Review* 41 (June 1976): 391–403.

Index

A

Adams, John Quincy: and Anti-Masonic Party, 54, 55
Africa: influence on black American institutions, 128–29; and oral history, 136
African Lodge No. 459: receives charter, 16–17; petitions for kidnapped blacks, 40; and first black public school, 41; membership of, 42; exclusion by Grand Lodge of Massachusetts, 68–69
Alexandria (Virginia): black Masons freed by white Masonic judges, 43
Allen, Richard: forms Free African Society, 28–29; founding father of black Freemasonry, 38; founder of African Methodist Episcopal church, 42; as Methodist minister and active Mason, 93
Alpha Kappa Alpha: founded at Howard University, 81
Alpha Phi Alpha: founded at Cornell University, 81
American Anti-Slavery Society, 93
Ancient York Masons: black group in Philadelphia, 42
Anti-Masonic party, 54, 59
Assimilationist model of American culture, 6

B

Bahamas: Prince Hall lodges in, 126
Bailyn, Bernard: on reasons for American Revolution, 13
Barbering: as black occupation, 27, 28
Barnett, Ross R.: as governor of Mississippi, 76
Basie, William ("Count"): famous Mason, 94
Batavia (New York): Morgan case and anti-Masonic feeling, 54–55

Benoit-Smullyan, Emile: on equilibrium in social change, 104
Bermuda: black lodges present since 1838 in, 44
Berlin, Ira: on experience of free blacks in the early nineteenth century, 21, 23–24, 26; emergence of black churches, 29; positive good theory of slavery, 34; diversity of black middle class, 112–13
Black middle class: and American Dream, 1; subject to status incongruity, 4–5; fraternal and other voluntary organizations, 5, 83; relation to larger black community, 37, 86
Blassingame, John: on importance of Freemasonry to blacks, 36–37
Boston: whites outraged by blacks calling themselves Freemasons, 14; Prince Hall and origins of black Freemasonry in, 16–17, 28; Prince Hall Masons hide charter on Commons, 17; blacks petition against slavery, 18; proposal to bar slaves from crafts, 33; first black public school in U.S., 41
Bradley, Thomas D.: famous Mason, 94
Brant, Joseph: Mohawk chief and Mason, 91
Brewster, Nero: petitions Massachusetts legislature for schools for black children, 41
Brown Fellowship Society, 79
Burial societies, 78

C

Calvinists: institutions in Dutch society, 7
Canada: Prince Hall lodges in, 126
Caste system: by race in U.S., 8, 132
Catholic church: Catholic institutions in Dutch society, 7; threatens excommunication of Freemasons, 64. See also Clement XII

Cayton, Horace: study of black community in Chicago, 83
Chalmers, David: analysis of ties between Ku Klux Klan and Masons, 76
Charleston (South Carolina): Brown Fellowship Society formed in, 79
Cherokee Indians: Mason adopted into tribe by chief, 91
Cherokee Lodge No. 21, 66
Chicago: fifteen Prince Hall lodges in 1885, 45. *See also* Drake, St. Clair
Chinese experience with Freemasonry, 67
Cincinnati: union president tried for apprenticing black, 22; racial relations in, 22–23, 34; leadership of black Freemasons in, 94
Clement XII:papal bull of 1738 against Freemasonry, 10–11
Cleveland: black members of white Masonic lodge in, 96
Colonization: discussed in black newspapers, 31; advocated by Massachusetts journal, 35
Colored Knights of Pythias, 79
Colorophobia of white Freemasonry, 6, 72
Congregation Beth B'nai Abraham: black synagogue, 93
Connecticut: and repressive racial laws during colonial period, 19
Conrad, George W.: builder and black Freemason, 94
Constitutional Convention: Masons among the members of, 12
Continental Army: accepts blacks as soldiers, 15
Cornell University: black fraternity founded, 81
Cornish, Samuel E.: editor of first black newspaper, 31
Crawford, George W.: on need of black Masons for white validation, 101

D

Dalton, Thomas: Prince Hall Mason active in abolition movement, 114
Daughters of Samaria: accepts blacks, 79
Davis, David Brian: on trends of nativistic literature, 56; Jacksonian fear of Masons, 57; attitude of Anti-Masons toward black Masons, 109

Declaration of Independence: Masons among the signers of, 12
Degler, Carl: on spread of Freemasonry during colonial period, 11
Delany, Martin: on irony of the freeborn convention, 71
Delta Sigma Theta: founded at Howard University, 81
Dollard, John: on strain experienced by middle-class blacks, 105
Douglas, Stephen A.: assists Mormon Masonic lodges, 66
Douglass, Frederick: criticizes black fraternity members, 84; questions black Masonic involvement, 111–12; warns against parallel institutions, 133
Drake, St. Clair: study of black community in Chicago, 83
Drayton, Paul: admitted to white lodge in South Carolina, 95
Dred Scott decision: restricts free blacks, 35
Du Bois, W. E. B.: on secret societies in Philadelphia's black community, 85
Dunmore, John Murray, Earl of: promises blacks freedom for enlisting in British army during American Revolution, 14
Durkheim, Emile: on social importance of symbols, 48
Dutch society: status and pillarization in, 6–7

E

Early, Joe: chef and black Mason, 94
Eliade, Mircea: on importance of initiation in premodern societies, 50
Elks of the World, Improved Benevolent Order of: founding of black Elks organization, 80–81
Ellington, Edward Kennedy ("Duke"): famous Mason, 94
Emancipation: in northern states, 31; effects of on blacks, 36
England: appeal of Freemasonry in, 10; use of blacks in British army, 14–15
Enlightenment: and decline of religion in America, 12
Episcopal church: Free African Society becomes first black Episcopal church, 29
Ethiopia: Prince Hall lodges in, 126

Index

Ethnicity versus assimilation, 6
Europe: discrimination in European Freemasonry, 99; Prince Hall lodges at American military bases in, 126

F

Faubus, Orval E.: as governor of Arkansas, 76
Feast of St. John's: confusion with name of Prince Hall lodge, 69
Fillmore, Millard: and Anti-Masonic party, 54
Fleming, Walter Millard: writes ritual for Nobles of Mystic Shrine, 52
Ford, Arnold Josiah: black rabbi and Mason, 93
Forten, James: leader in Negro Convention Movement, 93
Franklin, Benjamin, 11; defends Freemasonry in his Philadelphia newspaper, 53
Fraternities: black organizations begun, 81
Frazier, E. Franklin: on black associations, 82, 84; black stratification, 87; limitations of research on black middle class, 113; black politicians and fraternal organizations, 115
Free African Society, 29
Free blacks: legal and social position, 21–22, 29; size of population, 23, 26, 35; importance of organizations for, 23; type of land owned, 24; relationship with slaves, 25–26; beginning of black upper class, 27; antagonisms between northern freedmen and emancipated southerners, 27; southern restrictions against, 30; development of local newspapers for, 31; white reaction to, 32; entrepreneurial ventures with whites, 35
Freedmen's Bureau: superintendant objects to black Masons, 46
Freedom's Journal: first black newspaper, 31
Freemasonry, 3; racial separation in, 3, 5–6, 14, 72–74; relations with minority groups, 3, 47; extent of in colonial and revolutionary America, 10–12; as embodiment of gentility, 11; and religious toleration, 12; assistance given to black Masons by white

Freemasonry (Cont.)
Masons, 33, 40–41; philosophy of, 47–48, 49; medieval origins, 48; symbolism and ritual, 48–51; levels and systems of, 49, 51–52; stress on community responsibility, 52; government through the lodge, 52; opposition to, 53–59; Jews and European Masonry, 60–64; and conspiracy theories in Europe, 63–64; similiarity of Masonic and Mormon rituals, 65; and Native Americans, 66–67; and Chinese-Americans, 67; breach betweeen Ancient and Modern factions, 70; freeborn convention of, 70–71; ties to Ku Klux Klan, 76; black members of white lodges, 95–97; social interaction between black and white Masons, 97–98; as reference group for blacks, 107. *See also* Prince Hall Freemasonry
Fugitive Slave Act: increases racial tension, 35

G

Galilean Fishermen, 79
Georgia: repressive laws against free blacks, 29–30
Germany. *See* Traveler's Lodge No. 25
Gist, Noel P.: study of fraternalism, 137
Goldberg, Milton: on marginal culture, 106
Golden Fleece: location of first meeting place of black Freemasons in Boston, 16
Good Samaritans. *See* Independent Order of Good Samaritans and Daughters of Samaria
Gordon, Milton: on concept of ethnic subsociety, 111
Grand United Order of True Reformers, 78–79
Great Architect of the Universe: and principles of Freemasonry, 41
Goudsblom, Johan: and principle of pillarization in Dutch society, 6–7

H

Haiti: black expectations and the Haitian revolution, 28
Hall, Prince: revolutionary principles

Prince Hall (Cont.)
linked to freedom for blacks, 12– 14; petitions for admittance to white lodge, 14; obtains Masonic charter from England, 17; early life, 18; activist for black rights, 19, 38; Methodist clergyman, 19, 93; petitions for kidnapped blacks, 40; petitions for school for black children, 41; informs newspaper of mistake in name of black lodge, 69; correspondent to Mother Lodge of England, 69; attitude toward white Masons, 98

Hampton, Lionel: famous Mason, 94

Hancock, John: denies Prince Hall's suggestion that blacks be involved in colonists' struggle for freedom, 13

Harmony Lodge No. 5: expelled by Prince Hall grand lodge, 122

Hays, George W.: politician and black Mason, 94– 95

Hill, Lancaster: petitions Massachusetts legislature for schools for black children, 41

Hiram Grand Lodge of Pennsylvania: black rival to Prince Hall grand lodge, 122

Hiram Lodge No. 3: established in Rhode Island, 42

Holland. *See* Dutch society

Hooks, Rev. Benjamin L.: civil rights leader and Mason, 94

Hope, John H.: black member of white lodge in Cleveland, 96

Howard University: fraternities and sororities founded, 81

Hughes, Everett C.: on status dilemma of educated blacks, 104

Hyman, Herbert: and reference group theory, 107

I

Illinois: fifteen Prince Hall lodges in Chicago in 1885, 45

Independent Order of Good Samaritans and Daughters of Samaria: blacks accepted into, 79– 80

Indiana, University of: formation of black fraternity at, 81

Informer, The: editorial on lack of information on black Freemasonry, 135– 36

Irish Registry. *See* Lodge No. 441, Irish Registry

Isomorphism in black stratification, 103

J

Jackson, Maynard H.: mayor of Atlanta and Mason, 94

James, Daniel ("Chappie"): famous Mason, 94

Jews: and European Freemasonry, 60– 64; experience with American Freemasonry, 64; black Jewish congregation, 93

Jim Crow laws: system dismantled, 130– 31

Johnson, John: businessman (Ebony Corporation) and Mason, 94

Johnson, Melvin M.: on committee investigating status of Prince Hall lodge, 75

Jolly Corks: predecessor of American Elks, 80

Jones, Absolum: forms Free African Society, 28– 29; founding father of black Freemasonry, 38; and yellow fever epidemic, 40; Master of Philadelphia lodge, 42; Methodist clergyman, 93

Jones, Rev. Morgan: saved from Indians by Masonic signal, 91

Jordan, Winthrop: on anomaly of free blacks, 20

K

Kappa Alpha Psi: founded at University of Indiana, 81

Kendall, William B.: saves Prince Hall charter from fire, 17

Kentucky: whites help in formation of black lodge in, 95– 96

King, Martin Luther, 2

King David Lodge No. 5 of Havre de Grace: suppressed by white citizens in 1870, 119

Kirby Street Temple: meeting place of African Lodge No. 459 in Boston, 16

Knights of Tabor, 79

Ku Klux Klan: and white Masonry, 76

L

Lenski, Gerhard: on status inconsistency, 104

Lewin, Kurt: on the social reality function of groups, 88
Liberia: black Freemasons from Rhode Island migrate to, 42; Prince Hall lodges, in, 126
Lincoln, Abraham: and emancipation, 36
Lincoln (Nebraska): black community studied, 83
Lodge No. 441, Irish Registry: fifteen blacks initiated by Irish regiment in Boston, 14
Louisiana: status of free blacks in, 25
Louisville (Kentucky): black Freemasons freed by white Masons after raid, 43; United Brothers of Friendship and Sisters of the Mysterious Ten established, 79
Lynching: work of black Masons against, 116

M

McKisty, Col.: Mason saved from burning at the stake, 91
McManus, Edgar: on economic function of blacks, 34
McWilliams, Wilson Carey: on anti-Masonic feeling, 53; on transformation of Masons into Anti-Masons, 55
Manumission: increases free black population, 21
Marginality: positive and negative aspects of, 106
Maryland: fear of free blacks and their progress found in, 30
Marshall, Thurgood: a Prince Hall Mason, 94, 122; legal efforts supported by Prince Hall Masons, 121
Masonic Quarterly Review: on equality, 100
Masonic signal of distress, 41, 91
Masonry. *See* Freemasonry; Prince Hall Freemasonry
Massachusetts: Committee of Safety addressed by Prince Hall, 12–13; laws restricting blacks in, 24; highest investment in slave trade, 24; Grand Lodge of Massachusetts and recognition of Prince Hall Freemasons, 73–75, 77
Massachusetts General Colored Association: abolitionist society, 114

Merton, Robert S.: and status set theory, 108
Methodist church: Prince Hall becomes Methodist clergyman, 19; clergymen active in black Freemasonry, 93
Miller, David: newspaper editor involved in Morgan case, 54
Miller, Kelly: on attitude of educated blacks toward affiliation with whites, 102
Minority adjustment: example of Prince Hall Freemasonry, 4
Minority devaluation: emergence of black Freemasonry in response to, 9
Minstrel shows: originated by slaves and transformed by white showmen, 96
Mississippi: grand lodge severs Masonic relations with New Jersey Grand Lodge over admission of blacks, 46
Monroe, Frederic: presented medal by German Mason, 99
Morgan, William: kidnapping leads to anti-Masonic feeling, 54–55
Mormons: comparison of anti-Mormonism and anti-Masonic movement, 57; similiarity of Freemason rituals and Mormon religious ceremonies, 65; Mormon Masonic lodges, 65–66; discrimination of Masons against, 65–66
Mother Grand Lodge of England: grants charter to Prince Hall's lodge, 17; omits Prince Hall lodge in listing of world Masonry, 69; Prince Hall the sole American correspondent of, 69
Mt. Morah Lodge No. 1: members freed by white Masonic jailer, 43
Mt. Vernon Lodge No. 3: irregular origin comparable to African Lodge No. 459, 68
Mulattoes: distinction from other blacks, 25; and Brown Fellowship, 79
Muraskin, William A.: black Freemasonry as assimilationist response, 84; on negative feelings of black Masons toward black masses, 111; civil rights advocacy of black Masons, 116; on black Freemasonry and racism, 120; criticism of black Freemasonry, 120, 122; contends black Freemasonry teaches bourgeois social role, 126
Myrdal, Gunnar: on importance of black

Gunnar Myrdal (Cont.)
associations, 82; blacks as exaggerated
Americans, 83; sees black fraternities
as unimportant, 84; interpretation
questioned, 84, 113

N

National Association for the
Advancement of Colored People:
cooperation of black Masons, 117;
Legal Defense and Educational Fund
supported by black Masons, 121
Native Americans: experience with
Freemasonry, 66–67
Nazarites, 79
Nazi party: dissolves Masonic lodges in
Germany, 64
Negro College Fund: supported by
Prince Hall Masons, 121
Negro Convention Movement:
emergence in 1830s, 32; James For-
ten a leader of, 93
Netherlands. *See* Dutch society
New Albany (Indiana): Louisville Prince
Hall lodge meets in, 43
New England: repressive racial laws dur-
ing colonial period, 19; role in slave
trade, 24; antebellum population of
free blacks, 36
New Jersey: grand lodge accepts black
members, 46; black Masonic organi-
zation uses same name as white
Masonic body, 74
New York: grand lodge protests discrimination of Berlin Freemasons
against Jews, 63
New York Gazette: attack on Freemasonry in colonial times, 53
North Carolina: badge required for free
blacks, 29

O

Odd Fellows, International Order of:
black lodges of, 79–80
Odum, Howard: on importance of black
fraternal organizations, 84–85
Ogden, Peter: helps to establish black
lodge of Odd Fellows, 80
Olsen, Marvin: ethnic community
thesis, 83–84, 93

Omega Psi Phi: founded at Howard
University, 81
Oral history: use in study of Prince Hall
Freemasonry, 136
Orum, Anthony: on black social partici-
pation, 83

P

Park, Robert Ezra: on the black temperament, 90; advantages of marginality,
106
Pennsylvania: black Masonic lodge
breaks off from Prince Hall Masons,
122
Phi Beta Sigma: founded at Howard
University, 81
Philadelphia: first meeting of Negro
Convention Movement, 32; black
Freemasons aid victims during yellow
fever epidemic, 39–40; Prince Hall
lodge established, 42; white Masons
visit Prince Hall lodge, 43; colonial
newspaper accuses Masons of immorality, 53
Philomathean Lodge No. 646: first
black lodge of Odd Fellows, 80
Phoenix City (Alabama): service of
lodge to black community, 116
Pike, Albert: gives volume on Scottish
Rite to Prince Hall Mason, 74; as
Negrophobic Mason, 92
Pillarization: in Dutch society, 6–7; uses
for minorities, 7, 129; racial pillarization in U.S., 8–9; meaning for American society, 103; advantages and costs
of, 131–32; as analytical tool, 133;
European experience with, 134
Pittsburgh: blacks admitted to white
lodge by judge, 96–97
Pluralist model of American culture, 6
Port Royal (South Carolina): Mason
saved from Indians, 91
Positive good theory of slavery, 34
Prince Hall Freemasonry: and Masonic
ideology, 3–4, 108–9; advantages for
blacks, 4, 32–33, 40, 90–91; and
assimilationism, 4; as minority adjustment, 4–5, 9; attitude toward
white recognition, 6, 73, 100–101;
charter received, 17; Boston fire de-
stroys meeting place, 17; and black
community, 36–37, 94, 116–18;

Prince Hall Freemasonry (Cont.)
leadership of members, 38, 89, 92;
commitment to American values, 39;
and first black public school, 41; and
political change, 41–42, 114–16,
121–22, 129–30; spread of, 42, 44;
and Reconstruction, 44–45; irregular
status, 67–68; relations with Boston
Masons, 69, 72; and freeborn convention, 70–71; similiarity with black
Elks, 80; lack of visibility, 89, 118–
19; Methodist clergymen in, 93; relations with European Masons, 99; legal
research department established,
121; dissension within, 122–24; attractiveness to younger blacks,
124–25; functions and choices it provides, 127, 132; lack of records, 135;
significance of women's auxiliaries,
136. *See also* Freemasonry
Pyramid, The: newsletter of Prince Hall
Masons (Buffalo, N.Y.), makes no
mention of racism or integration, 101
Pythagorean groups: sponsored in high
schools by Prince Hall lodges, 125

R

Racial ascription: and black middle class,
5
Racial separatism, 6
Reconstruction: favorable time for black
Freemasonry, 44–45; role of black
lodges in, 115
Redding, Saunders: on welfare orienta-
tion of Prince Hall Masons, 41
Reference group theory, 107
Relative deprivation theory, 107–8
Revolution of 1848: effects on
Freemasonry, 63
Revolutionary War: use of blacks in
British and Continental armies,
14–15
Rhode Island: investment in the slave
trade, 24; Prince Hall lodge
established in, 42
Riggs, Arthur J.: establishes black Elks
organization, 80–81
Rose, Henry: issues permission for
Prince Hall Masons to practice Mason-
ic burial, 69
Rowe, John: grants permit to Prince
Hall to continue work of the craft, 16

Runciman, W. C.: on normative and
comparative reference groups,
99–100
Russworm, John B.: editor of first black
newspaper, 31

S

St. Bartholomew (West Indies): black
Freemason kidnapped to, 40
St. John's Lodge No. 50: suspended and
turned over to black members, 97
St. John's Lodge of Boston: blacks petition for admittance, 14
St. Louis (Missouri): integrated
cornerstone-laying ceremony in 1843
in, 97
Saunders, Prince: teacher at black
school in Boston, 41
Savannah (Georgia): skilled slaves hired
out by their masters, 34
Schlesinger, Arthur M.: on secret
societies and democracy, 59
Schomburg, Arthur: Prince Hall grand
historian, 98
Schooley, Charles A.: prominent Re-
publican and black Mason, 94
Scott, James: John Hancock's brother-
in-law, delivers charter to Prince Hall,
17, 68
Scottish Rite: system of Freemasonry,
51
Seeman, Melvin: on advantages of mar-
ginality, 106
Sharecroppers: class of blacks after the
Civil War, 36
Shays's Rebellion: and black expecta-
tions, 28; Prince Hall offers lodge
members to serve against, 39
Shriners: black group established in
Chicago, 52; black Shriners celebrate
civil rights decision, 120
Simmel, Georg: on secret societies, 44,
50, 137; loose structure of Masonry,
52; conflicts of marginality, 106
Simmons, Rev. William J.: Ku Klux
Klan organizer and active Mason, 76
Sisters of the Mysterious Ten: estab-
lished in Louisville, 79
Slave codes: in colonial New England,
19; free blacks subject to slave laws in
Georgia, 29
Slavery: compared with condition of

Slavery (Cont.)
American colonists, 13; role of New England colonies in the slave trade, 24; contacts between slaves and free blacks, 25; and the U.S. Constitution, 28; debate over its nature, 33

Smith, Joseph: Mormon leader, gives Masonic signal of distress before death, 92

Sororities: black organizations begun, 81

South Carolina: prohibition against assembly of free blacks, 30

Spanish America: dress regulations for free black women in Louisiana, 25

Springfield (Massachusetts): journal criticizes blacks, 35

Status inconsistency: and black middle class, 5, 104–5; black Freemasonry insulates against, 9; creates dissonance for black achievers, 87

Stevens, Thaddeus: anti-Masonic politician, 55

Stigmatization of American blacks, 5

Stratification: in American and Dutch societies, 8

Symbolic Degrees: system of Masonic ritual, 51–52

T

Tocqueville, Alexis de: on racial prejudice in northern states, 31

Traveler's Lodge No. 25 (Bitenberg, Germany): forms lodge in the Netherlands, 126

Truth, Sojourner, 2

Tubman, William: president of Liberia and a Mason, 94

Tuscarora Indians: sachem recognizes Masonic signal of distress, 91

Tuskegee Institute: supported by black Masons, 94

U

Underground railroad: and Prince Hall lodge in Washington, D.C., 114

Union Lodge of Albany (New York): origin comparable to that of African Lodge No. 459, 68

United Brothers of Friendship and Sisters of the Mysterious Ten: established in Louisville, 79

Urban League: Prince Hall Masons cooperate with, 117

V

Vansina, Jan: on African approach to oral history, 136

Veblen, Thorstein: on advantages of marginality, 106

Virginia: registration of free blacks required, 30

Voluntary associations: role in black community, 82–83

W

Wallace, George C.: as governor of Alabama, 76

War of 1812: proliferation of black churches during, 29

Washington, Booker T.: and expediency of Masonic affiliation, 93

Washington, George: Masonic membership of, 11

Washington, D.C.: Prince Hall lodge a part of the underground railroad, 114

Washington (State): grand lodge gives limited recognition to Prince Hall lodges, 73

Walker, David: 1830 appeal for military overthrow of U.S. government by blacks presented at Prince Hall temple, 114

Warren, Joseph: member of Massachusetts Committee of Safety, declines Prince Hall's request for involvement of blacks, 13

Weber, Max: on class differences among American blacks, 86; on status and power, 129

Weed, Thurlow: and Anti-Masonic party, 54

Wesley, Charles: on black business societies, 78; on black middle class, 85

West Indies: birthplace of Prince Hall, 18; free blacks kidnapped to, 40; West Indian emigrants form Brown Fellowship Society, 79; Prince Hall lodges in, 126

White, Judge J. W.: admits four blacks to Pennsylvania lodge, 97

Williams, Bert: and black musical theater, 96; white Masons render burial rites for, 96

Williamson, Harry A.: on blacks initiated into Masonry by British troops, 15; history of black Freemasonry, 74; on Prince Hall Masons and amalgamation, 100

Wilson, Dr. Leonidas: black member of white lodge in Cleveland, 96

Woodson, Carter: on antebellum number of professional blacks, 35; emphasis on the black tradition, 131

Wright, Rev. Theodore S.: Prince Hall Mason active in American Anti-Slavery Society, 93

Y

Yellow fever: black Masons help with care of the sick in Philadelphia, 39–40

York Masons. *See* Ancient York Masons

Young, Andrew: famous Mason, 94

Z

Ziegfield Follies: black actor joins, 96

Zuilen: social groups in Dutch society, 7